ONCE UPON A CERTAIN YEAR

ONCE UPON A CERTAIN YEAR

JOHNNIE LEE MOORE JR.

iUniverse, Inc.
Bloomington

ONCE UPON A CERTAIN YEAR

iUniverse books may be ordered through booksellers or by contacting:

iUniverse
1663 Liberty Drive
Bloomington, IN 47403
www.iuniverse.com
1-800-Authors (1-800-288-4677)

Because of the dynamic nature of the Internet, any web addresses or links contained in this book may have changed since publication and may no longer be valid. The views expressed in this work are solely those of the author and do not necessarily reflect the views of the publisher, and the publisher hereby disclaims any responsibility for them.

Any people depicted in stock imagery provided by Thinkstock are models, and such images are being used for illustrative purposes only.
Certain stock imagery © Thinkstock.

ISBN: 978-1-4620-3985-2 (sc)
ISBN: 978-1-4620-3987-6 (hc)
ISBN: 978-1-4620-3986-9 (ebk)

Printed in the United States of America

iUniverse rev. date: 11/30/2011

CONTENTS

CHAPTER 1

Once upon a certain year, there lived an old man by the name of Midas Dakota.
Midas had a wife named Rose, and together they lived in a small country town called Hawthornianville.

Midas and Rose loved the quiet peaceful town of Hawthornianville, especially when they got special visits from their beloved seven-year-old grandson named Tommy.

Tommy thought the world of his grandparents. He loved to hear great stories from them. They were full of wisdom, and Tommy loved to ask them a lot of questions, which they were always happy to answer.

One time Tommy's parents were going on a special one-week vacation cruise to celebrate their tenth year wedding anniversary. Unfortunately, they couldn't take Tommy with them. They needed someone whom they could trust to baby-sit and watch over Tommy. Who could they trust more than Tommy's favorite grandparents, Midas and Rose Dakota?

Tommy arrived at his grandparents' home on a Sunday afternoon, after his grandparents returned from church. Tommy's parents were good—hearted, loving people. But unfortunately, they both worked so much that they rarely had time to go to church. Therefore, Tommy thought that going to church was for special occasions, like Christmas and Easter. But his grandparents would change all of that.

After Tommy's parents left, Tommy helped his grandparents around the house with the chores before it was time for supper.

After eating supper, Rose and Midas wanted to relax and enjoy themselves by watching a little television. Tommy joined them on the sofa while they scanned the channels of the television set to see what they wanted to watch.

Finally, they stopped on a channel that was very familiar to them. This channel was showing an all day marathon of two of the special old time classics, Bewitched and I Dream of Jeannie.

Little Tommy watched a couple of episodes with his grandparents and became very impressed by what he saw. Because of the computer craze and modern day television, Tommy had never heard of these two classic shows. Therefore, they watched until it was time for bed.

Finally, before going to bed, little Tommy had many questions to ask his grandparents. "Who had more powers, Samantha or Jeannie?" "Who was prettier, Samantha or Jeannie?" Who is older, and which show came on first?" "Who played Samantha and Jeannie?" "Who is older in real life; are they still alive?"

All those questions, Midas and Rose tried to answer the best way they could.

"Samantha and Jeannie were a little different in personality and style. Yet, because of their similarities, they would always be linked and compared with each other," Rose answered.

Little Tommy was truly amazed that these two legendary women were almost the exact same age, and that their shows ran almost at the exact same time.

"I can tell you this," Midas said, "Barbara Eden and Elizabeth Montgomery were actually one calendar year apart in age, but there were a couple of significant people in our history, who were likewise often compared with one another in real life; people who were born the exact same year; people who had different styles, yet same missions; people who rose to the top of their field at about the same time."

"Oh really, please tell me who?" Tommy begged. "Oh please, please, please tell me."

"Okay, I'll tell you a story," Midas answered, finally giving in to Tommy's pleas. "But you must first promise me that you will go straight to bed."

"I promise," Tommy answered.

After they said their prayers, Midas tucked Tommy into his bed and gave him this bedtime story:

Once upon a certain year, when Lyndon B. Johnson was President of the United States, there were born two babies who would grow up to be perhaps two of the greatest hip-hop rap artists-turned actors of all time, with the younger of the two being the greater of the two.

In the city of Bayshore, Long Island, was born a baby by the name of James Todd Smith. Several months later, in the city of Philadelphia, Pennsylvania, was born a baby by the name of Willard Christopher Smith, Jr.

They both started rapping at a very young age. The rapping revolution started in the mid 1970's, and both James and Willard were inspired by what they heard.

Before he became a rapper, little James Todd spent most of his time singing in the church choir, while little Willard used his charming and sly demeanor to become the class clown in school. Such a behavior earned him the nickname, "Prince." Unfortunately, little James Todd turned to rap music to emotionally escape the violent and troublesome relationship of his parents.

At the age of twelve little James was rapping in studios. It was at this moment that he came to be known as LL Cool J, an acronym for Ladies Love Cool James. LL Cool J bought a lot of hip-hop records to get the label's address so he could send in his demo tapes. One of the companies he sent one of his demo tapes to was Def Jam Records. After listening to his demo tape, Def Jam immediately signed LL. Shortly thereafter he released his first record, entitled, Radio in 1985.

While still in his teens, young Will Smith met a young man by the name of Jeffery Towns.

The two immediately hit it off, and D. J. Jazzy Jeff and the Fresh Prince were born, with Will Smith doing the rapping and Jeff Towns controlling the music.

Throughout the late 1980's, both LL Cool J, and D. J. Jazzy Jeff and the Fresh Prince ascended to the top elite of all the rap artists with hits like, "I Can't Live Without My Radio," "I'm Bad," "I Need Love," "Girls Ain't Nothing But Trouble," "Nightmare on My Street" and

"I Think I Can Beat Mike Tyson."

In the late 1980's, rap music became so popular, that they decided to add a rap category at the Grammy Awards, with Will Smith earning hip-hop's very first Grammy.

Unlike most of the hip-hop rap artists who followed them, both LL Cool J and the Fresh Prince were two of the few rap artists who didn't have to use profanity to sell their records.

This is an epitome in itself, which set them apart from the rest.

By the time the 1990's rolled around, both LL and the Fresh Prince discovered that their incredible talents were far beyond rap music. LL was the first one out the gate with his cameo appearance in the movie, Krush Groove in 1985.

Likewise, Will Smith hit immediate stardom in the field of acting with the popular hit television show "The Fresh Prince of Bel-Air." LL Cool J shortly followed the same path with a similar hit television show of his own called, "In The House." Both men had the privilege of working with the talented actor, Alfonso Ribeiro, who was a co-star of both series.

Although they both reached a pinnacle that very few rap artists before them had ever reached, both Will Smith and LL Cool J would show the world why their acting talent was much bigger than television. Will Smith enjoyed success with mega hits like Bad Boys I and Bad Boys II, Men in Black I and Men in Black II, Independence Day, Enemy of the State, Ali, and The Pursuit of Happiness. LL Cool J hit it big with movies like Deep Blue Sea, Any Given Sunday, Charlie's Angels, Kingdom Come, Roller Ball, Deliver Us from Eva, and S.W.A.T.

Along with Ice T and Ice Cube, the two became the greatest hip-hop rapper-turned—actor talent of all time.

But unlike the previous two, these two men, both Will Smith and LL Cool J, were born in the exact same year.

Among the best actors of his generation, Will Smith proved that his talent was something to be reckoned with. Twice he was nominated for Best Lead Actor in a motion picture film for his respective roles in the movies, Ali and The Pursuit of Happiness, losing out only to Denzel Washington and Forrest Whitaker.

Both James Todd Smith and Will Smith have won numerous awards in the three major entertainment medias : movies, television and music. And with both being very young, there is a good chance that their best days are yet to come.

In conclusion you may find many people who can make the claim of having enjoyed similar success, but not too many have had the privilege of being born the same year. That's why no one else in their field can be compared to them.

They were the greatest in their field: born the same year, and ascending to the top at the exact same time.

The End

CHAPTER 2

The very next morning, little Tommy got up bright and early with joy.

"Wow, that was a great story you told me last night, Grandpa," he said.

"I know, I know," Grandpa answered. "Now go wash, brush your teeth and freshen up for breakfast."

After he brushed his teeth, Tommy was still jubilant with a radiant smile. "I never realized how much two people could change the whole world," he said.

"Well, it's true," Grandpa answered. "They both changed the world in their own distinctive ways."

"Do you think that one day I can change the world like that?" Tommy asked.

"Anything is possible, if you put your heart and mind to it," Grandpa answered.

"But how would I know what God wants me to be?" Tommy asked.

"When the time is right, you will know."

Little Tommy stood before his Grandpa with a pondering expression on his face.

After a brief moment of silence, he exhaled and said, "I think I want to grow up to be a hip-hop rap artist."

Cautiously amazed to hear little Tommy say that, Midas Dakota answered, "Well, if that is your sincere dream, then go for it. But like I said, when the time is right, you will know. Just pray and ask God about it, then wait on Him. He will give you an answer."

Shortly thereafter, little Tommy joyfully gathered himself together at the breakfast table with his grandparents.

"What's for breakfast?" he asked, while letting the dainty smell of the breakfast aroma engulf his nostrils."

"Biscuits, syrup, oatmeal and orange juice," Grandma answered with a smile.

"Oh wee, I just love your biscuits, syrup, oatmeal and orange juice," Tommy answered with joy.

After saying their grace, little Tommy and his grandparents delighted themselves with a very delicious breakfast.

After breakfast, Tommy helped his grandma plant in the garden, and then he helped his grandpa plow the field. When they were finished with their chores for the day, little Tommy spent the remainder of the day playing around the house. The more he played, the more he started wishing and hoping that he could one day grow up to become a hip-hop rap artist.

Later that night, after they ate supper and watched a little television, it was time for bed.

"Please tell me another bedtime story. Oh please, please, please tell me a bedtime story," Tommy begged his grandfather.

"Okay, I'll tell you another story," Grandpa answered. "But once again, you have to promise me that you will go straight to bed."

"I promise," Tommy answered.

After they said their prayers, Grandpa Midas tucked Tommy into his bed and gave him this bedtime story:

Once upon a certain year, when John F. Kennedy was President of the United States, there were born two babies who would grow up to be perhaps the two greatest basketball players of the 1990's, if not the two greatest of all time, with the younger of the two being the greater of the two.

In the city of Lagos, Nigeria, in the country of Africa was born a baby by the name of Hakeem Abdul Olajuwon. One month later, in the city of Brooklyn, New York, was born a baby by the name of Michael Jeffrey Jordan.

They both emerged on the national basketball scene as promising freshmen in the 1982 NCAA Final Four, with Jordan's North Carolina Tarheels topping Olajuwon's Houston Cougars in the semifinals before going on to defeat a Patrick Ewing—led Georgetown Hoyas in a classic battle in which Jordan made the winning shot.

Before he was introduced to basketball, young Hakeem was an outstanding soccer player, while Michael tried to play basketball, football, and baseball. His love and passion for baseball later led him to decide to retire from basketball while still at the height of his prime so he could pursue a career in major league baseball.

In high school, unfortunately, Michael was cut from the basketball team as a sophomore. But the following summer he worked hard and trained vigorously and established himself as a dominant player.

At about the same time, 15-year-old Hakeem played his very first basketball game and immediately picked up on the game tremendously.

While Michael earned a major basketball scholarship to play for the University of North Carolina under the legendary coach, Dean Smith, Hakeem was only merely offered a visit to the University of Houston for a work out for Coach Guy Lewis.

Impressed by what they saw, the coaching staff immediately made plans for the seven foot tall Hakeem to emigrate from Africa. He improved his skills by going head to head with NBA MVP Moses Malone of the Houston Rockets, in pick-up games.

While in college, both Michael and Hakeem established an NCAA Championship rivalry with superstar Patrick Ewing, with Jordan winning in 1982 and Olajuwon falling a little short in 1984.

Hakeem never won a championship in college, but his play was so dominant, he was named the 1983 NCAA Tournament Most Valuable Player of the Year. No one since, from a losing team, has ever been bestowed that honor.

Teamed with superstar Clyde Drexler, Hakeem's Cougars were affectionately known as the Phi Slama Jama, because of their outstanding dunking abilities.

After leading the Houston Cougars to three straight final four appearances and two straight championship games, Hakeem decided to turn pro. Once again, Hakeem found himself being linked to Michael Jordan, who decided to turn pro also, setting up a very talented class for the 1984 NBA draft. Olajuwon was picked first overall by the Houston Rockets, while the Chicago Bulls took Jordan third overall. Both players had outstanding Rookie years. As a Rookie, Michael Jordan averaged 28.2 points per game, while Hakeem Olajuwon, still known as Akeem at the time, averaged 20.6 points, 11.9 rebounds, and 2.68 blocks. Olajuwon teamed up with the seven foot four Ralph Sampson to form a dominating tandem known as the Original Twin Towers. Together they improved the Rockets win total by 19 games. Both Michael and Hakeem lived up to their rookie expectations, with Michael winning the Rookie of the Year Award, and Hakeem finishing second.

Jordan's second season was cut short by a broken foot, which caused him to miss 64 games. Yet he still came back in time for the playoffs. Although his Bulls were swept by the high—powered Boston Celtics who were led by superstar Larry Bird, Jordan put together one of the greatest displays in NBA playoffs history by scoring a record 63 points in a single game.

In the same playoffs, Olajuwon made a name for himself, by leading the Rockets to shock the defending NBA Champions, Los Angeles Lakers, by easily defeating them four games to one, with Olajuwon outplaying superstar Kareem Abdul-Jabbar. Although they made an indomitable effort in the finals, the Rockets fell in six games to the highly favored Celtics.

Throughout the late 1980's, both Jordan and Olajuwon continued to make a name for themselves, winning numerous awards, like the MVP in 1988 for Jordan and the epic 1988 slam dunk contest that he won over the great Dominique Wilkins. Yet it was the 1990's when both Jordan and Olajuwon elevated their dominance to another level by becoming the most feared players both offensively and defensively.

From 1991 until 1998, the Chicago Bulls and the Houston Rockets were the only two teams to win the NBA Championship. And from that same period, no other player was named NBA Finals MVP, but Jordan and Olajuwon.

Both players had great footwork ability that made it very difficult for their opponents to defend against them.

Jordan was simply unstoppable and Olajuwon was famous for his signature Dream Shake move that left some of the best defenders misdirected and frozen in their tracks.

In the years of Michael Jordan's championship run, he went head to head with some of the best guards in the game, like Isiah Thomas, Magic Johnson, Clyde Drexler, Gary Payton and John Stockton, leaving no doubt who was the greatest.

In the years of Hakeem Olajuwon's championship run, he went head to head with some of the best centers in the game, like Patrick Ewing, David Robinson and Shaquille O'Neal, leaving no doubt who was the greatest.

Charles Barkley, Patrick Ewing and Karl Malone are perhaps three of the greatest players of all time, who never won an NBA Championship. In some of their best legitimate playoff efforts, it was either a team led by Jordan or Olajuwon that deprived them of obtaining a championship.

Another interesting thing about Jordan and Olajuwon is how they both elevated their game in the playoffs against the two who succeeded them as MVP in the 1993 and 1995 regular seasons, respectively.

Charles Barkley had the best year of his career in winning the Most Valuable Player Award in the 1993 regular season. Yet, when he went head to head against the 1992 MVP Jordan in the 1993 Championship, Jordan's amazing performance proved to Barkley and the rest of the world that Jordan was still the MVP.

David Robinson had the best year of his career in winning the Most Valuable Player award in the 1995 regular season. Yet, when he went head to head against the 1994 MVP Olajuwon in the 1995 Western Conference Championship, Olajuwon's amazing performance proved to Robinson and the rest of the world that Olajuwon was still the MVP.

Unfortunately, in the eight-year reign of these two MVPs, they never met in the playoffs. Such a meeting could have been compared to the Bird-Magic rivalry, if not the Russell-Chamberlain rivalry.

But unlike the other rivalries, these two were born in the exact same year, and began their NBA careers the same year.

Because of Olajuwon's great NBA career, very few people have criticized the Houston Rockets for picking him ahead of Jordan, like they do the Portland Trailblazers for picking Sam Bowie.

To name a few of their many accomplishments, both were named among the fifty greatest players in NBA history. Both are Olympic gold medalists, with Jordan winning it twice, first as a collegiate, then as a member of the Original NBA Dream Team. Jordan is a five time MVP, while Olajuwon won his lone MVP award in 1994.

Olajuwon is a two time Defensive Player of the Year, while Jordan won his lone Defensive Player of the Year in 1988.

Jordan won the NBA Scoring Title a record ten times.

Olajuwon was the only player in NBA history to win MVP, Finals MVP and Defensive Player of the Year in the same season.

Jordan is the all time leader in steals.

Olajuwon is the all time leader in block shots.

Jordan has the all time career scoring average.

Olajuwon is the only player in the top ten on the career list in scoring, rebounding, block shots, and steals. Jordan won the finals MVP a record six times.

Olajuwon is one of only four players in NBA history ever to record a quadruple double.

And both are at least a twelve time NBA All-Star.

In conclusion, you may find many people who can make the claim of having enjoyed similar success, but not too many have had the privilege of being born the same year. That's why no one else in their field can ever be compared to them.

For they were the greatest in their field: born the same year and ascending to the top, at about the exact same time.

The End

CHAPTER 3

The very next morning, little Tommy got up bright and early with joy.

"Wow, that was a great story you told me last night, Grandpa," he said.

"I know, I know," Grandpa answered. "Now go wash, brush your teeth, and freshen up for breakfast."

After he brushed his teeth, Tommy was still jubilant with a radiant smile, "I never realized how much two people could change the whole world," he said.

"Well, it's true," Grandpa answered. "They both changed the world in their very own distinctive ways."

"Do you think that one day I can change the world like that?" Tommy asked.

"Anything is possible, if you put your heart and mind to it, Grandpa answered.

"But how would I know what God wants me to be?" Tommy asked.

"When the time is right, you will know.

Little Tommy stood before his grandpa with a pondering expression on his face. After a brief moment of silence, he

exhaled and said, "I think I want to grow up to be a basketball player."

Cautiously amazed to hear little Tommy say that, Midas Dakota answered, "Well if that is your sincere dream, then go for it. But like I said, when the time is right, you will know. Just pray and ask God about it, then wait on Him. He will give you an answer."

Shortly thereafter, little Tommy joyfully gathered himself together at the breakfast table with his grandparents.

"What's for breakfast?" he asked, while letting the dainty smell of the breakfast aroma engulf his nostrils.

"Pancakes, eggs, bacon and milk," Grandma answered with a smile.

"Oh wee, I just love your pancakes, eggs, bacon and milk," Tommy answered with joy.

After saying their grace, little Tommy and his grandparents delighted themselves with a very delicious breakfast.

After breakfast, Tommy helped his grandma feed the chickens, and then he helped his grandpa feed the farm animals. When they finished their chores for the day, little Tommy spent the remainder of the day playing around the house. The more he played, the more he started wishing and hoping that he could one day grow up to become a professional basketball player.

Later that night, after they ate supper and watched a little television, it was time for bed.

"Please tell me another bedtime story. Oh please, please, please tell me a bedtime story," Tommy begged his grandfather.

"Okay, I'll tell you another story," Grandpa answered. "But once again, you have to promise me that you will go straight to bed."

"I promise," Tommy answered.

After they said their prayers, Grandpa Midas tucked Tommy into his bed and told him this bedtime story:

Once upon a certain year, when Dwight D. Eisenhower was President of the United States, there were born two babies who would grow up to be the two greatest musical pop icons of the

1980's, if not two of the greatest of all time, with the younger of the two being the greater of the two.

In the city of Minneapolis, Minnesota, was born a baby by the name of Prince Rogers Nelson. Several months later, in the city of Gary, Indiana, was born a baby by the name of Michael Joseph Jackson.

Both Prince and Michael's fathers were great gifted musicians. Therefore, it is no surprise that the musical talents were something that they both inherited.

Prince was named after his father's Jazz band, which was called the Prince Rogers Trio.

Michael Jackson was the first one out of the gate when he was discovered, and became famous with the Jackson 5, who later became known as The Jacksons.

Although he became a star as both a soloist and as the lead singer of those groups, Michael didn't yet establish himself as a mega superstar until the 1980's.

Prince, who also became a mega superstar in the 1980's, didn't become nationally known until many years after Michael.

Throughout the 1980's there was an undisputed two-way battle between these men as the most dominant pop artist of the decade, if not of all time.

Before he became a star, little Prince formed a band called Grand Central, which he formed while he was in junior high school.

By the mid-seventies, Prince was able to play over twenty different musical instruments. While traveling in local arenas, his musical talents were discovered by Warner Brothers, who immediately signed him to a contract.

Michael Jackson, who had enjoyed great success with Motown, was never given the creativity and control of his music. Because of this, and other reasons, he and all his brothers, except Jermaine, decided to leave Motown and sign a contract with a CBS record label called Epic Records.

Prince's first album, entitled For You, was released in 1978.

By this time, Michael had released an album with his brothers, entitled Destiny. Plus, he was starring in a movie, along with Diana Ross, called The Wiz.

The movie was an urban remake of the old classical movie, The Wizard of Oz, in which Michael played the Scarecrow, and Diana Ross played Dorothy.

The songs for the movie were arranged by Quincy Jones, who later got together with Michael about the idea of producing Michael's first solo album with Epic Records.

When 1980 came, both Prince and Michael were ascending their way toward the top of the music kingdom. Prince enjoyed hits like, I Wanna Be Your Lover, and Controversy, while Michael's Off The Wall album became the first album ever to spawn four top ten hits.

This album signaled the arrival of a new Michael Jackson, who was not dependent upon his brothers to further his career.

In 1982, Michael Jackson's second solo album Thriller became the biggest selling album of all time, while becoming the first in history to spawn seven top ten hits.

The popular television video channel, MTV, for a long time didn't show regular airplay of black musical artists, but the musical influence of Michael Jackson was so great that he became one of the pioneers that broke the color barrier on MTV, with the videos Beat It and Billie Jean. In the dawn of the musical video generation, Michael Jackson forever changed the way music videos would be made, and his videos Thriller and Beat It are still considered two of the greatest musical videos ever made.

The album Thriller spent an amazing 37 weeks at the number one spot on the charts, and over 122 weeks on the charts altogether.

1982 was also the year that Prince released his breakthrough album, entitled 1999. With smash hits like the album's namesake(1999), and Little Red Corvette, 1999(the album) sold over three million copies.

In 1983, Michael Jackson already undisputedly stood alone at the top of the music world, but when he appeared on Motown 25 and did his signature-dancing move called the moonwalk, he definitely orbited himself into the musical stratosphere.

This momentum carried on into 1984. His Michaelmania popularity was so great that it was obvious whom the mass of people came to the White House to see when Jackson received an invitation from President Ronald Reagan.

While filming a Pepsi Cola commercial, there was a technical malfunction that caused fire to spark which ignited Michael's hair. He was rushed to the hospital with severe burns. Yet, he recovered in time to receive a record breaking eight Grammy Awards.

Toward the end of 1984, it was evident that only Prince was capable of slowing down Michael's momentum. He released an album entitled Purple Rain to coincide with a movie that he filmed by the same name.

When the song Purple Rain reached number one on the charts, Prince simultaneously held the spot of number one film, number one single and number one album at the same time, with all three categories bearing the same name. The album also spawned other smash hits like, When Doves Cry and Let's Go Crazy. The album Purple Rain sold more than 13 million copies, while the film Purple Rain grossed more than $80 million. Prince won a couple of Grammys for Purple Rain, as well.

Although Prince didn't win as many Grammys as Michael Jackson, he did something that Michael never accomplished. He won an Oscar at the Academy Awards for Best Original Score for Purple Rain.

By early 1985, Prince's status was just as great as Michael's and the ego of the two apparently couldn't dwell in the same room when a group of talented artists gathered to record the song We Are The World. The occasion was a USA for Africa charity to help raise money to feed starving African children. For undisclosed reasons, Prince, who was suppose to sing a verse immediately following Michael's verse, decided to send Sheila E to represent him.

Sheila E sung along in the background vocals, while Prince's lead verse was given to Henry Lewis of the Henry Lewis and the News. The song, which was written by Michael Jackson and

Lionel Richie, won a Grammy, and was the best selling single of the 1980's.

In 1987, the two biggest pop stars of the eighties once again came close to collaborating together on another project. Michael Jackson talked with Prince about performing a duet together for Michael's upcoming Bad album. However, due to creative differences, the idea was canned and Michael had to record the single Bad on his own.

As for the album, although it didn't match the sales of Thriller, Bad sold over 32 million copies worldwide.

Throughout the 80's, their music became so popular that they were often referred to as the Prince and the King of Pop.

If they weren't busy writing hits for themselves, they were busy writing hits for other artists such as The Time Band, Vanity 6, Sheila E, Apollonia 6, Chaka Khan, Sinead O'Connor, Tina Turner, Rockwell and Diana Ross.

Toward the end of the 80's, their dominant status decreased a little and ironically was threatened by another person born in the same year of their birth: a woman by the name of Madonna. However, peculiar as they were, these two men were still the undisputed two-way rulers of the decade, if not of all time.

In conclusion, you may find many people who can make the claim of having enjoyed similar success, but not too many have had the privilege of being born the same year. That is why no one else in the field can ever be compared to them.

For they were the greatest in their field: born the same year, and ascending to the top, at about the exact same time.

The End

CHAPTER 4

The very next morning, little Tommy got up bright and early with joy.

"Wow, that was a great story you told me last night, Grandpa," he said.

"I know, I know," Grandpa answered. "Now go wash, brush your teeth, and freshen up for breakfast."

After he brushed his teeth, Tommy was still jubilant with a radiant smile. "I never realized how much two people could change the whole world," he said.

"Well, it's true," Grandpa answered. "They both changed the world in their very own distinctive way."

"Do you think that one day I can change the world like that?" Tommy asked.

"Anything is possible, if you put your heart and mind to it," Grandpa answered.

"But how would I know what God wants me to be?" Tommy asked.

"When the time is right, you will know," Grandpa answered.

Little Tommy stood before his Grandpa with a pondering expression on his face. After a brief moment of silence, he

exhaled and said, "I think I want to grow up to be a singer and musician."

Cautiously amazed to hear little Tommy say that, Midas Dakota answered, "Well, if that is your sincere dream, then go for it. But like I said, when the time is right, you will know. Just pray and ask God about it, then wait on Him. He will give you an answer."

Shortly thereafter, little Tommy joyfully gathered himself together at the breakfast table with his grandparents.

"What's for breakfast?" he asked, while letting the dainty smell of the breakfast aroma engulf his nostrils.

"French toast, eggs, sausage, and milk," Grandma answered with a smile.

"Oh wee, I just love your French toast, eggs, sausage, and milk," Tommy answered with joy.

After saying their grace, little Tommy and his grandparents delighted themselves with a very delicious breakfast.

After breakfast, Tommy helped his grandma pick plums and peaches, and then he helped his grandpa mow the grass. When they finished their chores for the day, little Tommy spent the remainder of the day playing around the house. The more he played, the more he started wishing and hoping that he could one day grow up to become a professional singer and musician.

Later that night, after they ate supper and watched a little television, it was time for bed.

"Please tell me another bedtime story. Oh please, please, please tell me a bedtime story," Tommy begged his grandfather.

"Okay, I'll tell you another story," Grandpa answered. "But once again, you have to promise me that you will go straight to bed."

"I promise," Tommy answered.

After they said their prayers, Grandpa Midas tucked Tommy into bed and gave him this bedtime story:

Once upon a certain year, when Jimmy Carter was President of the United States, there were born two babies who would grow up to be perhaps two of the greatest fierce rivals in the game of Women's Tennis, with the younger of the two, being the greater of the two.

In the city of Lynwood, California was born a baby by the name of Venus Ebone Starr Williams. Several months later, in the city of Kosice, Czechoslovakia was born a baby by the name of Martina Hingis.

There were greater on-court rivalries, like Chris Evert and Martina Navratilova, but unlike those two who became good friends, the rivalry of Williams and Hingis was unique because they constantly had a lot of verbal jabs off the court to go along with their fierce competition on the court.

They both started playing tennis at a very young age under the influence of their parents, who were also their coaches.

In 1993, the era of Chris Evert and Martina Navratilova was over, and the game of tennis suffered a terrible crisis when Monica Seles, who was a potential rival to Steffi Graf, was attacked from behind by a deranged fan. The game of tennis desperately needed a new era of saviors.

Enter Martina Hingis and Venus Williams, who both turned professionals in the exact same month of October, in the exact same year of 1994.

Before Hingis turned pro, she wasn't just winning all of the junior events, she was dominating all of the junior events, mainly defeating a potential future rival by the name of Anna Kournikova, who was born one year later than Martina Hingis. Venus Williams, on the other hand, didn't play junior tennis.

Nevertheless, she improved her game by practicing and playing against someone who was also born one year later, her baby sister, Serena Williams.

After they turned pro, Venus was held back by her father to play in only two or three tournaments per year, while Hingis' mom allowed her to compete in as many tournaments as possible.

Hingis stormed out of the gate, winning matches, and setting a record as the youngest player to accomplish something significant. In 1996, Hingis became the youngest Wimbledon Champion when she teamed up with Helena Sukova to win the

Women's Double Championship. With enough matches under her belt, toward the end of 1996, Martina Hingis established herself as a formidable potential rival to both Steffi Graf and Monica Seles.

When 1997 arrived, Hingis made it clear that she was the undisputed number one women's tennis player in the world. She became the youngest Grand Slam Singles Winner in history when she won the Australian Open by defeating former champion Mary Pierce. Although she won almost every tournament she entered, Hingis failed to win the French Open, losing in the Finals to Iva Majoli. Nevertheless, Hingis rebounded at Wimbledon, and continued setting records, when she became the youngest Wimbledon Singles Champion ever by defeating the grass court specialist Jana Novotna.

Coincidentally, while Hingis was busy dominating, 1997 was the first time Venus Williams played tennis on a full time basis. The result was the beginning of a rivalry when Venus Williams stormed all the way to the U. S. Open Championship to face the world's number one, Hingis. Martina easily won the title 6-0, 6-4, yet Venus made a statement and sent a message that this was just the beginning of more grand slam showdowns to come.

By 1999, the world of tennis expected a four-way rivalry, with Anna Kournikova and Serena Williams, who both were a year younger, to be added to the mix. But Kournikova never lived up to her expectations in singles, and Hingis was left alone to take on both Williams' sisters by herself. A perfect example was the 1999 U. S. Open in which Martina Hingis defeated Venus Williams in an epic semifinal showdown, only to lose to Serena Williams in the finals.

However, the four did meet in a classic 1999 French Open doubles championship with the Williams sisters defeating Martina Hingis and Anna Kournikova 6-3, 6-7, 8-6, in what was a thrilling match.

Both Venus Williams and Martina Hingis have enjoyed winning numerous doubles Championships. Martina won nine double titles, teaming up with Kournikova on a few occasions.

Venus won six double titles, teaming up with her sister Serena each time.

In 1998 Martina won all four doubles championships, giving her the rare grand slam in doubles. 1998 was also the year in which one Williams' sister won every mixed doubles championship, with Venus triumphing in the Australian Open and French Open, and Serena winning the Wimbledon and U. S. Open mixed double titles.

Despite a few interruptions by Lindsay Davenport, Martina Hingis held the number one ranking for an amazing total of 152 weeks from 1997-2001, until Jennifer Capriati finally replaced her.

Ironically, it was Venus Williams who replaced Capriati as the number one player in the world.

How fitting, Venus Williams', road toward her first grand slam singles title ran through the five-time grand slam champion, Martina Hingis. In a very competitive Wimbledon quarterfinals match, Venus defeated Martina 6-3, 4-6, 6-4, before going on to defeat her sister Serena in the semi finals and Lindsay Davenport in the championship to claim the title.

The quarterfinals victory over Hingis was a boost to Williams' confidence. She went on an amazing winning streak afterwards, winning the U. S. Open Title and an Olympic Gold Medal in the process.

Before winning the U. S. Open against Lindsay Davenport, Venus had another epic semifinal showdown against Martina, in which her amazing comeback from defeat was totally incredible.

Not only did Venus win an Olympic Gold Medal in singles, she teamed with her sister Serena and won the Olympic Gold Medal in doubles.

Toward the end of the year 2000, Martina Hingis was still the number one player in the rankings, but Venus Williams was clearly the number one player on the court.

In 2001, Martina was determined to regain that momentum edge. In the process, she became the first woman to defeat both Williams sisters in the same grand slam tournament. She did so when she defeated Serena, then Venus, respectively in the quarterfinals, and semifinals of the Australian Open.

For number one ranked Hingis to defeat one Williams sister was a challenge, let alone defeating both. Unfortunately for Martina, to accomplish that amazing task and then have the red-hot American prodigy Jennifer Capriati waiting for her in the finals was overwhelming. As a result, Capriati claimed her first grand slam title by defeating Hingis in a thriller.

In 2001 Venus defended her Wimbledon and U. S. Open titles against two future dominating players. At Wimbledon she defeated the upstart Justine Henin. During the trophy presentation after her victory, Venus Williams, who was often criticized for being just as cocky as Hingis, was very gracious in praising and predicting Justine Henin's bright future.

At the U. S. Open in New York, Venus defeated her sister Serena Williams on September 8, 2001, just three days before the September 11 attacks. Finally in 2002, Venus Williams officially became the number one ranked player in the world.

In 2003, injuries forced both Martina Hingis and Venus Williams to spend time off the tennis court, thus allowing other players to catch up and pass them in the rankings.

Nevertheless, when at their best, and injury free, no other players were more dominant with a fierce rivalry than Martina Hingis and Venus Williams. Both have won at least five grand slam singles. Only Serena Williams and Justine Henin have won more since 1997.

But unlike the other two, these two champions were born in the exact same year, and began their careers in the exact same year.

Both Martina and Venus have earned at least 18 million dollars in prize money. They both have won over four hundred career matches, and they both have won over thirty-five titles. Head to head, their records are almost evenly matched. Hingis won three Australian Opens, one Wimbledon and one U. S. Open, while Williams won five Wimbledons and two U. S. Opens.

With both players still being very young, and if they can avoid major injuries and distractions, they both still have a legitimate chance of adding to their career titles and, of course, continuing their fierce rivalry.

In conclusion, you may find many people who can make the claim of having enjoyed similar success and rivalries, but not too many have had the privilege of being born the same year. That is why no one else in their field can ever be compared to them. For they were the greatest in their field: born the same year, and ascending to the top at about the same time.

The End

CHAPTER 5

The very next morning, little Tommy got up bright and early with joy.

"Wow, that was a great story you told me last night, Grandpa," he said.

"I know, I know," Grandpa answered. "Now go wash, brush your teeth, and freshen up for breakfast."

After he brushed his teeth, Tommy was still jubilant with a radiant smile. "I never realized how much two people could change the whole world," he said.

"Well, it's true," Grandpa answered. "They both changed the world in their very distinctive way."

"Do you think that one day I can change the world of men's tennis like that?" Tommy asked.

"Anything is possible, if you put your heart and mind to it," Grandpa answered.

"But how would I know what God wants me to be?" Tommy asked.

"When the time is right, you will know," Grandpa answered.

Little Tommy stood before his grandpa with a pondering expression on his face. After a brief moment of silence, he

exhaled and said, "I think I want to grow up to be a Pro Tennis player."

Cautiously amazed to hear little Tommy say that, Midas Dakota answered, "Well, if that is your sincere dream, then go for it. But like I said, when the time is right, you will know. Just pray and ask God about it, then wait on Him. He will give you an answer."

Shortly thereafter, little Tommy joyfully gathered himself together at the breakfast table with his grandparents.

"What's for breakfast?" he asked, while letting the dainty smell of the breakfast aroma engulf his nostrils.

"Grits, toast, eggs, ham and milk," Grandma answered with a smile.

"Oh wee, I just love your grits, toast, eggs, ham and milk," Tommy answered with joy.

After saying their grace, little Tommy and his grandparents delighted themselves with a very delicious breakfast.

After breakfast, Tommy helped his grandma water the flowers and roses, and then he helped his grandpa rake the yard. When they finished their chores for the day, little Tommy spent the remainder of the day playing around the house. The more he played, the more he started wishing and hoping that he could one day grow up to become a professional male tennis player.

Later that night, after they ate supper and watched a little television, it was time for bed.

"Please tell me another bedtime story. Oh please, please, please tell me a bedtime story," Tommy begged his grandfather.

"Okay, I'll tell you another story," Grandpa answered. "But once again, you have to promise me that you will go straight to bed."

"I promise," Tommy answered.

After they said their prayers, Grandpa Midas tucked Tommy into his bed and gave him this bedtime story:

Once upon a certain year, when Franklin D. Roosevelt was President of the United States, there were born two babies who would grow up to be perhaps two of the greatest martial artists of all time, with the younger of the two being the greater of the two.

In the city of Ryan, Oklahoma, was born a baby by the name of Carlos Ray Norris. Several months later, in the city of San Francisco, California, was born a baby by the name of Bruce Lee. Together they single handedly put martial arts on the map and influenced millions of others to follow in their footsteps.

Before he studied martial arts, Chuck Norris was a poor little non-athletic shy kid who was neglected by his alcoholic father. His parents divorced when he was ten and little Chuck and his two brothers moved with their mom to California.

Because of his half Indian heritage, little Chuck, who was still known as Carlos at the time, was often teased and taunted by his peers. He often dreamed of learning how to fight so he could beat up on his teasers.

Bruce Lee, on the other hand, through his father, was introduced to film at a very young age. By the time he was eighteen, he had appeared in over twenty films, while living in Hong Kong. Bruce was also introduced to martial arts by his father. He started when he was about twelve years old, learning under the Wing Chun Master, Yip Man.

The young Bruce was also thoroughly trained in western boxing, plus he developed the technique of fencing from his brother Peter Lee, who was a champion fencer. These different fighting styles helped Bruce to become extraordinarily great.

The turning point for both men came when they were eighteen years old.

At 18, Chuck Norris graduated from high school and joined the United States Air Force. His first military mission was in South Korea. It was in South Korea where he began training in the karate form of Tang Soo Do. Chuck's skills quickly improved in his training, and he advanced his way toward becoming a black belt.

As the 1958 Boxing Champion in Hong Kong, the young Bruce received a lot of challenges when he was 18. One of those challenges came from the son of a feared triad gang member. Bruce beat him so badly that Bruce's father became worried about his safety. He greatly feared that the triad gang would seek revenge on Bruce's life. As a result, he decided to send the young Bruce to the United States.

In the United States, Bruce enrolled at the University of Washington, in Seattle, Washington. He was a drama major, plus he took some philosophy classes.

In 1962, Chuck Norris had completed his duties in the Air Force and returned to California. At that time, Bruce Lee had finished college, and immediately they both opened up their own martial arts schools, attracting many students, including famous celebrities.

In the early sixties, Bruce Lee was so focused on his martial arts and fitness training that he didn't really have time to think about acting in films. That would soon change, however, when television producer William Dozier was impressed when he saw Bruce Lee's demonstration at the 1964 Long Beach Karate tournament. He immediately decided to hire Bruce to play Kato in the new television show called The Green Hornet.

Although the series lasted for only one year, it gave Bruce the chance to show millions of viewers his excellent kung fu skills. His character was so incredible the producers thought it would be a good idea for Bruce to appear in a couple of episodes of Batman.

After a slow start, Chuck Norris became so great that he won virtually every karate tournament he entered. He avenged every defeat he suffered by easily defeating the likes of Louis Delgado and Joe Lewis. In fact, it was after a championship victory over Joe Lewis, when he first met and became friends with Bruce Lee.

After going through vigorous competition, there was nothing that Chuck Norris wanted more than a good night's sleep. Yet after Bruce Lee approached him and introduced himself, his vibrant conversation re-energized Chuck Norris, and the two talked for hours. That first meeting was the start of a friendship, which included a lot of sparring battles and workouts.

Alone with their amazing martial arts skills, both men strongly believed in being physically fit. Chuck Norris won a lot of competitions because his physical fitness was vastly superior to his opponent's. His physical training was so popular throughout the years that he later became the face and spokesperson for the exercise equipment called Total Gym. Every year thousands of people buy and work out with the Total Gym, all because of the inspiration of Chuck Norris.

Bruce Lee's workout technique was an inspiration to millions of people, as well. A lot of famous bodybuilders were jealous of Bruce Lee's physique, especially his abdominal muscles. Bruce Lee believed that the abdominal muscles were one of the most important muscle groups for a martial artist because they protect your ribs and vital organs like a shell; plus, every movement requires some degree of abdominal work.

Along with his extraordinary skills, it was Bruce's body conditioning that made him incredibly hard to defeat. His speed was so fast; he could snatch a dime out of a person's open palm and replace it with a penny before the person could close it. His strength was so powerful he could knock a 200 lb opponent fifteen feet backwards with a one-inch punch. His accuracy was so precise he could throw a portion of food high into the air, and then catch it in mid-flight with his chopsticks, before putting it in his mouth. Any opponent who has such a combination of tremendous speed, power, and accuracy would always be hard to defeat.

Both Bruce Lee and Chuck Norris took their traditional style of learning and expanded it into their own style. Chuck Norris created the Chun Kuk Do, which was based primarily on the Tang Soo Do that he learned, yet it included elements from every combat style he learned. Bruce Lee created the Jeet Kune Do, which was based primarily on the Wing Chun that he had learned, yet it included elements from every combat style he had learned. The two even learned a lot from each other.

Although he could perform almost every imaginable kick, Chuck Norris was famous for his spinning kick and round house kick. Although Bruce was able to perform every kick, he was famous for his leaping fly kick, crescent kick, and thrusting side kick. Among other things, Bruce Lee was also famous for his great ability to use the nun chucks at a very high speed, for doing push-ups with only his thumb and index finger, his immortal cat call, and of course, taking his shirt off while engaged in a combatant battle.

Both men were often imitated but never duplicated. The two were able to become good friends because they both admired and respected one another's incredible talent.

Being impressed with Chuck Norris' ability to act, even before Chuck himself knew he had the ability to act, Bruce Lee was credited for helping Chuck Norris get his first film role in a movie called The Wrecking Crew. Chuck Norris would years later become one of the best actors in Hollywood, making numerous movies and starring in the popular hit television series, Walker Texas Ranger.

With many films under his belt, Bruce Lee made many efforts to get a major role in several Hollywood films. Yet because of his Chinese heritage, he was constantly turned down. Hurt and disappointed by this, Bruce Lee returned to Hong Kong, and soon found out that he was very famous in Hong Kong because of his role in the Green Hornet. Because of Bruce, they referred to it as the Kato Show.

Movie producer, Raymond Chow hired Bruce to play in the movie, Fist of Fury, which became a huge box office success. Next for Bruce was the Chinese Connection which was more successful than the Fist of Fury.

At that time, tragedy had struck in both Bruce Lee's and Chuck Norris' lives. Bruce lost his father, and also his Kung Fu mentor, Yip Man, while Chuck's younger brother Weiland Norris was killed in the Vietnam War. Chuck would later dedicate his Missing in Action movies in his brother's memory.

Being a professional middleweight karate champion for six consecutive years without a defeat, Chuck Norris was in a class above all of his challengers.

When Bruce Lee decided to make his third film, Return of the Dragon, he immediately called on America's best, Chuck Norris, and together they made perhaps the best fight scene in film history. Bruce Lee went on to make two more films, Enter the Dragon, which was finally produced by a Hollywood Studio, and the Game of Death.

Enter the Dragon was a bigger success than all of his previous films but unfortunately, Bruce never had the chance to see the movie's success, nor was he able to complete filming the Game of Death.

In mid-July of 1973, Chuck Norris received a phone call from Bruce, who flew to California from Hong Kong. Bruce wanted to get together with Chuck and have dinner; Chuck agreed. At dinner, Bruce told Chuck why he was in town. He told him that he was having black outs and he came to Los Angeles to get better treatment from better doctors. He also told Chuck that the doctors couldn't find anything wrong with him.

"They said I have the insides of an 18 year old," Bruce told Chuck.

Shortly after that dinner with Chuck Norris, Bruce Lee flew back to Hong Kong. Unfortunately, within a week, he would be dead. Chuck Norris was one of the many who attended Bruce's funeral. He was one of Bruce's pallbearers.

Within a year, Chuck Norris retired as Karate Champion. Shortly thereafter, he started acting. His first starring role was in the 1977 film, Breaker, Breaker. Throughout the years he made such successful movies as, A Force of One, The Octagon, Lone Wolf McQuade, Code of Silence, Delta Force I, Delta Force II, and of course the Missing in Action trilogy.

In addition, he started the anti-drug program called, Kick Start, which is still effective today.

In conclusion, you may find many martial artist who can make the claim of having enjoyed similar success, but not too many have had the privilege of being born the same year. That is why no one else in their field can ever be compared to them, for they were the greatest in their field: born the same year, and ascending to the top at about the exact same time.

The End

CHAPTER 6

The very next morning, little Tommy got up bright and early with joy.

"Wow, that was a great story you told me last night, Grandpa," he said.

"I know, I know," Grandpa answered. "Now go wash, brush your teeth, and freshen up for breakfast."

After he brushed his teeth, Tommy was still jubilant with a radiant smile. "I never realized how much two people could change the whole world," he said.

"Well, it's true," Grandpa answered. "They both changed the world in their very own distinctive way."

"Do you think that one day I can change the world like that?" Tommy asked.

"Anything is possible, if you put your heart and mind to it," Grandpa answered.

"But how would I know what God wants me to be?" Tommy asked.

"When the time is right, you will know."

Little Tommy stood before his Grandpa with a pondering expression on his face. After a brief moment of silence, he exhaled and said, "I think I want to grow up to be a martial arts master."

Cautiously amazed to hear little Tommy say that, Midas Dakota answered, "Well, if that is your sincere dream, then go for it. But like I said, when the time is right, you will know. Just pray and ask God about it, then wait on Him. He will give you an answer."

Shortly thereafter, little Tommy joyfully gathered himself together at the breakfast table with his grandparents.

"What's for breakfast?" he asked, while letting the dainty smell of the breakfast aroma engulf his nostrils.

"Milk and cereal, ham and cheese croissant, and orange juice," Grandma answered with a smile.

"Oh wee, I just love your milk and cereal, ham and cheese croissant, and orange juice," Tommy answered with joy.

After saying their grace, little Tommy and his grandparents delighted themselves with a very delicious breakfast.

After breakfast, Tommy helped his grandma with the laundry, and then he helped his grandpa paint the house. When they finished their chores for the day, little Tommy spent the remainder of the day playing around the house. The more he played, the more he started wishing and hoping that he could one day grow up to become a martial arts master.

Later that night, after they ate supper and watched a little television, it was time for bed.

"Please tell me another bedtime story. Oh please, please, please tell me a bedtime story," Tommy begged his grandfather.

"Okay, I'll tell you another story," Grandpa answered. "But once again, you have to promise me that you will go straight to bed."

"I promise," Tommy answered.

After they said their prayers, Grandpa Midas tucked Tommy into his bed and gave him this bedtime story:

Once upon a certain year, when Harry S. Truman was President of the United States, there were born two babies who would grow up to be the first two Presidents of the 21st century, with the younger of the two being the greater of the two.

In the city of New Haven, Connecticut, was born a baby by the name of George W. Bush. One month later, in the city of Hope, Arkansas, was born a baby by the name of William Jefferson Blyth, III. They were both named after their fathers, with little William changing his last name to Clinton after his stepfather, because his biological father died before he was born.

They both started their political careers by running for the House of Representatives, in which they both were defeated. Yet they both had successful terms as governor, before becoming President.

Before he become President, little George W. Bush was the head cheerleader at Phillips Academy, an all boys school, while little William J. Clinton was an accomplished saxophone player in the Hot Springs High School Band.

Young George was inspired by his father, George H.W. Bush, and grandfather, Prescott Bush to become a public figure, while young William, who would simply be known as Bill, used President John Kennedy and Martin Luther King Jr., as his main inspiration.

They both graduated from Yale University. George earned a degree in history in 1968 before joining the Texas Air National Guard, while William obtained a Juris Doctor degree from Yale Law School, after becoming a Rhodes Scholar at Oxford University.

George W. Bush later became a successful businessman in Oil and baseball, briefly owning the Texas Rangers of the Major League Baseball, while Bill Clinton briefly was Attorney General in Arkansas.

As Presidents, they were the first two Presidents of the 21st century and the new millennium, with Clinton being the only President ever to have the magnificent feat of having his term over—lap two different millennia.

Clinton won his Presidential elections in two electoral blowouts, while Bush won in two of the closest elections in Presidential history, losing the popular vote in 2000.

Despite the controversial election of 2000, Bush obtained a presidential record of 90% approval rating immediately after his strong leadership in the wake of the September 11 attacks. And despite the partisan Republican—controlled Congress impeachment of Clinton, he still left office with a 65% approval rating, the highest of any end of Presidency since World War II.

On October 21, 1994, the Clinton-Gore administration launched the first official White House website.

Both Clinton and Bush broke the traditional choice of picking middle—aged white men to fill their cabinet posts, thereby giving women and minority men hope of obtaining high positions.

Clinton was the first to break the tradition with such names as Janet Reno, Ronald Brown, Federico Pena and Hazel O'Leary.

Bush followed his lead with choices like Carlos Gutierrez, Ann Veneman and Alberto Gonzales.

Under Clinton, Madeleine Albright became the first woman ever to be appointed Secretary of State, the highest cabinet post under the President and Vice President.

Under Bush, Colin Powell became the first African American ever to be appointed Secretary of State, and later Condoleeza Rice became the first African American female ever to hold that position.

And another interesting thing, both Clinton and Bush became the first two sitting Presidents to visit the Fort Polk-Leesville, Louisiana, area, the home of novelist Johnnie Lee Moore Jr. Both men served a total of 16 years, making it the first time two men of two different parties served 8 years back to back.

Right or wrong, Bush was admired by many for his unshakeable belief and tough stance, despite mounting criticism, while Clinton was admired by many for his genius approach in restoring the nation's poor economy and creating millions of new jobs in the booming 1990's.

Federal Reserve Chairman, Alan Greenspan, who was loyal to the Republican party and had served under many Presidents, stated that President Clinton, who was a Democrat, was the smartest and most intelligent President that he had ever known.

Inheriting a poor economy, Clinton miraculously turned the nation's economy around. He presided over the longest period of peacetime economic expansion in American history, which included a balanced budget and a federal surplus.

Despite the bad choices that Clinton made with health care reform and extra marital affairs, he made some significant contributions such as the Family and Medical Leave Act, the Brady Bill, and Earned Income Tax Credit, the Minimum Wage Increase Act, and the Omnibus Budget Reconciliation Act of 1993.

Despite the bad choices that Bush made with the weapons of mass destruction, Hurricane Katrina, and dealing with the high gasoline prices, he made some significant contributions such as the $1.3 trillion tax cut, the No Child Left Behind Program, and of course, the War on Terrorism.

In conclusion, you may find many Presidents who can make the claim of having been born the same year, but not too many have had the privilege of being born the same year, and serving in the new millennium. That is why no one else in their field can ever be compared to them. For they were the greatest in their field: born the same year, and ascending to the top at about the exact same time, the new millennium.

The End

CHAPTER 7

The very next morning, little Tommy got up bright and early with joy.

"Wow, that was a great story you told me last night, Grandpa," he said.

"I know, I know," Grandpa answered. "Now go wash, brush your teeth, and freshen up for breakfast."

After he brushed his teeth, Tommy was still jubilant with a radiant smile. "I never realized how much two people could change the whole world," he said.

"Well, it's true," Grandpa answered. "They both changed the world in their very own distinctive way."

"Do you think that one day I can change the world like that?" Tommy asked.

"Anything is possible, if you put your heart and mind to it," Grandpa answered.

"But how would I know what God wants me to be?" Tommy asked.

"When the time is right, you will know."

Little Tommy stood before his Grandpa with a pondering expression on his face. After a brief moment of silence, he

exhaled and said, "I think I want to grow up to be the President of the United States."

Cautiously amazed to hear little Tommy say that, Midas Dakota answered, "Well, if that is your sincere dream, than go for it. But like I said, when the time is right, you will know. Just pray and ask God about it, then wait on Him. He will give you an answer."

Shortly thereafter, little Tommy joyfully gathered himself together at the breakfast table with his grandparents.

"What's for breakfast?" he asked, while letting the dainty smell of the breakfast aroma engulf his nostrils.

"Biscuits and gravy, egg omelet, toast and milk," Grandma answered with a smile.

"Oh wee, I just love your biscuits and gravy, egg omelet, toast and milk," Tommy answered with joy.

After saying their grace, little Tommy and his grandparents delighted themselves with a very delicious breakfast.

After breakfast, Tommy helped his grandma do some grocery shopping in town, and then he helped his grandpa go fishing at the lake. When they finished their chores for the day, little Tommy spent the remainder of the day playing around the house. The more he played, the more he started wishing and hoping that he could one day grow up to become President of the United States.

Later that night, after they ate supper and watched a little television, it was time for bed.

"Please tell me another bedtime story, oh please, please, please tell me a bedtime story," Tommy begged his grandfather.

"Okay, okay, I'll tell you a story," Grandpa answered.

"It has to be about two people who were greater than the Presidents," Tommy said.

"I am afraid that I can't think of anyone straight off hand," Grandpa answered.

"But you just gotta tell me another one," Tommy answered. "You just gotta."

"I am sorry, but I can't think of anyone else who was born the same year, who had greater magnitude of contributions than these," Grandpa answered.

"Oh please, please, please," Tommy begged.

Rose Dakota listened while her husband struggled to accommodate little Tommy's request.

"Okay, I'll tell you a bed time story," she said after she intervened.

"Will you?" Tommy asked.

"Yes, and we will save the best for last," she answered. "It is about two people who were far greater than what you have heard so far. The people whom your grandpa told you about were great, but greater is He that is in you than he that is in the world."

"Who is this person that is in me?" Tommy asked.

"His name is Jesus," Grandma answered.

"I thought Jesus lives in heaven?" Tommy said.

"He does, but He also enjoys living inside of all of us. For our body is His holy temple." Grandma answered.

"What other person was born the same year as Jesus?" Tommy asked.

"When is Jesus' birthday?" Grandma asked back.

"Christmas day," Tommy answered with joy.

"Well, if that's true, then this other person, who was six months older, had to be born the same year," Grandma answered.

"Who was this other person?" Tommy asked.

"His name was John the Baptist," Grandma answered.

"Why does everybody call him John the Baptist?" Tommy asked.

"Because God sent him to baptize people and to prepare their hearts for Jesus," Grandma answered.

"Was John the Baptist just as great as Jesus?" Tommy asked.

"No," Grandma answered. "Just like all the other stories Grandpa told you, the younger of the two was the greater of the two. Jesus was before John, but He was born into this world after John, making Him the younger of the two. Jesus is so great and powerful that He even created the men who created Superman, Batman, Spiderman and the Hulk. As you already know, Jesus is the Son of God. But John was greater than everyone else because he was the greater born of a woman, according to Jesus.

"Unlike the other great people, these two focused on our souls. For what will it profit a man to gain the whole world and lose his soul?"

"Could you tell me more about Jesus and John the Baptist?" Tommy asked.

"Yes," Grandma answered. "Just like all the people that your grandpa told you about, these two were not a fairy tale. They were real people, and Jesus is still real, living in our hearts."

"I go to church and learn on Christmas and Easter, but can you tell me more?" Tommy asked.

"Yes, but first you must promise me that you will go straight to bed." Grandma said.

"I promise," Tommy answered.

After they said their prayers, Rose tucked Tommy into his bed and gave him the greatest bed time story ever told.

Once upon a certain year, when Herod the Great was king of Judea, there were born two babies who would grow up to be the two greatest born of a woman, with the youngest of the two being the greater of the two.

In the temple of God, the Lord sent the Angel Gabriel to a priest name Zecharias to tell him about John the Baptist.

"For he shall be great in the sight of the Lord, and shall drink neither wine nor strong drink; and he shall be filled with the Holy Ghost, even from his mother's womb," the Angel told Zecharias concerning his son John.

Six months later, in the city of Nazareth, God sent the Angel Gabriel to a virgin named Mary to tell her the good news about the Savior, Jesus Christ.

"And Behold, thou shalt conceive in thy womb, and bring forth a son, and shalt call his name Jesus. He shall be great, and shall be called the Son of the Highest: and the Lord God shall give unto Him the throne of His Father David: and he shall reign over the house of Jacob forever; and of his kingdom there shall be no end," the Angel told Mary concerning her son Jesus.

Zecharias and Mary both were afraid when they saw the Angel Gabriel, but he told them not to be afraid.

Because Zecharias didn't believe the Angel, he wasn't able to speak again until after the baby John was born.

After the Angel told Mary that both she and her older cousin Elizabeth, Zacharias' wife, were pregnant, she immediately went to visit Elizabeth. When she did, baby John was so happy that he leaped for joy, while still inside his mother's womb.

Joseph, Mary's husband, couldn't understand how Mary became pregnant. Therefore, he wanted to get rid of her privately. But the Angel Gabriel spoke to him in a dream and said, "Joseph, thou son of David, fear not to take unto thee Mary thy wife; for that which is conceived in her is of the Holy Ghost, and she shall bring forth a son, and thou shalt call his name Jesus: for He shall save his people from their sins."

Because of Caesar Augustus' tax decree, Joseph and Mary were forced to travel all the way from Nazareth to Bethlehem during her pregnancy.

In Bethlehem, because there was no room for them in the inn, little Jesus was born in a manger, wrapped in swaddling clothes.

"Glory to God in the highest and on earth peace, goodwill toward men," said the Angels to the shepherds, who in response said, "Let us now go even unto Bethlehem, and see this thing which is come to pass, which the Lord hath made known to us."

The wise men, who also sought him, asked the question, "Where is he that is born King of the Jews? For we have seen His star in the east, and are come to worship Him."

When Herod the king heard these things, he was troubled, and all Jerusalem with him. Herod ordered all the babies who were up to two years old to be killed, but God warned Joseph and Mary, and they safely took Jesus to Egypt until the death of King Herod.

Immediately, young John and young Jesus knew the purpose of their calling. John grew up in the wilderness, living off of locusts and wild honey, while young Jesus knew that He must be about His Father's business.

When the time came, John started preaching and baptizing in the river of Jordan, beyond the wilderness, preparing the way for Jesus.

Although Jesus later testified and gave John the ultimate praise, John knew that he was no comparison to Jesus when he said, "I indeed baptize you with water unto repentance, but he that cometh after me is mightier than I, whose shoes I am not worthy to bear; He shall baptize you with the Holy Ghost, and with fire."

Again, when John the Baptist was asked whether or not he was the Christ, he answered,

"I am not the Christ, I am the voice of one crying in the wilderness, make straight the way of the Lord. But there standeth one among you, whom ye know not; He it is, who coming after me is preferred before me, whose shoe's latchet I am not worthy to unloose."

John was right; Jesus was before him, because He is the beginning and the ending, The Son of God.

For when the time had come to redeem mankind from their sins, Jesus said, "Prepare me a body because burnt offerings and sacrifices thou O Father have no pleasure. For behold, I come to do Thy will, O God." And He was speaking about John the Baptist when He said, "Behold, I will send my messenger, and he shall prepare the way before me."

When Jesus came to be baptized by John, John replied and said, "I have need to be baptized of Thee, and comest Thou to me?" Yet Jesus answered and said, "Allow it to be so now: for thus it becometh us to fulfill all righteousness."

And when John baptized Him, the heavens opened, and the Spirit of God descended upon Jesus like a dove. Immediately a voice from heaven said, "This is my beloved Son, in whom I am well pleased.

After Jesus was baptized, He went into the wilderness and prayed and talked with God for forty straight days and nights, without having either food or drink.

After the forty days were over, naturally Jesus was hungry. The devil knew that Jesus was hungry, so he tried to tempt

Jesus by saying, "If you are the Son of God, command that these stones be made bread."

Jesus rebuked him and answered, "It is written; man shall not live by bread alone, but by every word that proceedeth out of the mouth of God."

Again the devil tried to get Jesus to jump off the top of a temple by saying, "It is written, He shall give His angels charge over you, and in their hands they shall catch you, lest you dash your foot against a stone."

But Jesus answered again and said, "It is also written, Thou shalt not tempt the Lord thy God."

The devil, who had gotten Eve and the first Adam to sin by using his now famous three fold deception—an invitation to eat a forbidden food, the false assurance of not dying when you disobey the will of God, and the belief that he could use something pleasant to the eyes to cause you to think you can be as wise as God without serving Him—had failed in his first two attempts with Jesus, whom the Bible refers to as the second Adam. Now the devil was ready for his third trick.

So determined to trick Jesus, the devil took Him to a high mountain and showed Him all the glorious kingdoms of the world, then said, "All these things will I give you, if you will bow down and worship me." But unlike Adam and Eve, Jesus rebuked him again and said, "Get out of here, Satan! For it is written, you shall worship the Lord your God, and Him only shall you serve." Immediately, the devil left Him alone and the angels came to serve Jesus everything that he needed.

When starting their ministry, the very first message that both Jesus and John the Baptist preached was, repent, for the kingdom of heaven is at hand.

One day when John saw Jesus walking by, he said, "Behold the Lamb of God, which taketh away the sin of the world; this is He of whom I said after me cometh a man which is preferred before me; for He was before me, and I knew him not: but that He should be made manifest to Israel, therefore am I come baptizing with water. "I saw the Spirit of God descend from heaven like a dove, and abode upon Him. For God told me upon whom you shall see my Spirit descend, the same is He which baptizes with the Holy Ghost, and I saw and bore record that this is the Son of God."

Some of John's disciples followed Jesus. "We have found Him of whom Moses and the prophets wrote about, Jesus of Nazareth, the Son of Joseph," Philip joyfully told his brother Nathaniel. "Can anything good come out of Nazareth?" Nathaniel asked. "Come and see," Philip answered. When Jesus revealed to Nathaniel that he knew everything about him, Nathaniel doubted him no more, as he proclaimed, "Rabbi, Thou art the Son of God; Thou art the King of Israel!" Jesus let him know that he would witness greater things, like the angels from heaven ascending and descending upon the Son of Man. Many of John the Baptist's disciples started following Jesus, including Andrew, who was Simon Peter's brother, yet there were some who wanted to remain loyal to John.

John answered his disciples by saying, "A man can receive nothing, except it be given him from heaven. You yourselves are my witness that I said, 'I am not the Christ, but that I am sent before Him.' He that has the bride is the bride groom: but the friend of the bridegroom, which standeth and heareth Him, rejoiceth greatly because of the bridegroom's voice; this, my joy therefore is fulfilled. He must increase, but I must decrease. He that comes from above is above all; He that is of the earth is earthly and speaketh of the earth; he that comes from heaven is above all. And what He has seen and heard, that He testifieth; and no man receives His testimony. He that hath received His testimony hath set to His seal that God is true. For He whom God hath sent speaketh the words of God; for God giveth not the Spirit by measure unto Him. The Father loveth the Son, and hath given all things into His hand. He that believeth on the Son hath everlasting life; and he that believeth not the Son shall not see life; but the wrath of God abideth on Him."

Jesus Himself confirmed John's testimony when He said to Nicodemus, "And no man hath ascended up to heaven, but He that came down from heaven, even the Son of man which is in heaven. And as Moses lifted up the serpent in the wilderness, even so must the Son of man be lifted up: That whosoever believeth in him should not perish, but have eternal life. For

God so loved the world, that He gave His only begotten Son, that whosoever believeth in Him should not parish, but have everlasting life. For God sent not his Son into the world to condemn the world; but that the world through him might be saved. He that believeth on Him is not condemned; but he that believeth not is condemned already, because he hath not believed in the name of the only begotten Son of God."

At that time Galilee was ruled by a king named Herod Antipas. He was an heir of Herod the Great. He had a brother named Philip. John the Baptist told Herod Antipas that he did wrong by marrying his brother's wife. This woman's name was Herodias. She hated John for disapproving of her marriage to Herod. She wanted John dead. Herod captured John the Baptist and put him into prison, but he feared killing John because he knew that many people regarded John as a prophet.

After John was locked up, a mass of people followed Jesus. When Jesus saw the multitude of people following Him, He went up to a mountain and taught them saying, "Blessed are the poor in spirit; for theirs is the kingdom of heaven. Blessed are they that mourn; for they shall be comforted. Blessed are the meek; for they shall inherit the earth. Blessed are they which do hunger and thirst after righteousness; for they shall be filled. Blessed are the merciful; for they shall obtain mercy. Blessed are the pure in heart; for they shall see God. Blessed are the peace makers; for they shall be called the children of God. Blessed are they which are persecuted for righteousness sake; for theirs is the kingdom of heaven. Blessed are ye, when men shall revile you, and persecute you, and shall say all manner of evil against you falsely, for my sake. Rejoice, and be exceedingly glad; for great is your reward in heaven; for so persecuted they the prophets which were before you." Jesus had love and compassion on the multitude that followed Him.

At one time He fed them with only two little fish and five loaves of bread.

Jesus also loves the little children. Red, yellow, brown, black or white, we are all precious in His sight. When his disciples tried to prevent the little children from coming to Jesus, He rebuked them and said, "Allow the little children to come to me, and don't stop them; for of such is the kingdom of God, verily I say unto you, whosoever shall not receive the kingdom of God as a little child, he shall not enter there in."

There was a group of religious people called the Pharisees. They didn't believe in Jesus, especially when he told a paralyzed man that his sins were forgiven. When the Pharisees murmured and complained, Jesus answered and said, "Which of the two is easier to say, your sins are forgiven, or to say arise and walk?" The Pharisees were speechless; therefore Jesus continued and said, "So that you may know the Son of man has power on earth to forgive sins," then He said to the paralyzed man, "Arise, pick up your bed and go home." Immediately the paralyzed man was able to walk. When the crowd saw what happened, they glorified God for giving such powers to Jesus.

Nevertheless, the Pharisees still did not believe. Neither could they understand why Jesus would heal a centurion's servant, or sit and eat with a tax collector. Jesus answered and said, "If I do not the works of my Father, believe me not, but if I do, though you believe not me, believe the works that you may know, and believe the Father is in me, and I in Him."

Jesus told his disciples that the scribes and Pharisees sit in Moses' seat, therefore listen to what they say, but don't do what they do. Jesus knew that they did things to be seen of men, instead of sincerely pleasing God. Therefore in comparison, he said that the publican went home more forgiven that the Pharisee who exalted himself and became abased, while the sinful publican humbled himself and allowed God to exalt him. Time after time Jesus proved His identity to the Pharisees, but they still wouldn't believe.

Locked up in prison, even John the Baptist wanted a final assurance of Jesus' identity. He sent two of his disciples to Jesus and asked, "Are you He that should come, or do we look for another?" Jesus answered and said, "Go and show John again those things which you do hear and see; the blind receive their sight and the lame walk, the lepers are cleansed, and the deaf hear, the dead are raised up, and the poor have the gospel preached to them. And blessed is he, whosoever shall not be offended in me."

After John's disciples left, Jesus gave John the ultimate praise when He said to His followers, "What did you go out into the wilderness to see, A prophet? Yes, I say unto you, and more than a prophet, for this is He, of whom it is written, Behold, I send my messenger before thy face, which shall prepare thy way before thee. Verily I say unto you, among them that are born of women, there hath not risen a greater than John the Baptist; notwithstanding He that is least in the kingdom of heaven is greater than he.

"And from the days of John the Baptist until now the kingdom of heaven suffereth violence; and the violence take it by force. For all the prophets and the law prophesied until John. And if ye will receive it this is Elijah, which was to come. He that hath ears to hear, let him hear; but whereunto shall I liken this generation?

"It is like unto children sitting in the markets, and calling unto their fellows, and saying, we have played the pipe for you, and you did not dance; we have mourned unto you, and you have not lamented. For John came neither eating nor drinking, and they say, He hath a devil. The Son of man came eating and drinking and they say, behold a glutton and a winebibber, a friend of tax collectors and sinners. But wisdom is justified of her children."

Shortly thereafter, Herod Antipas had a birthday party. He invited a host of friends and leaders. At the party, the daughter of Herodias danced before Herod and his guests. So pleased with her dancing, Herod promised with an oath to give her whatever she would ask for.

The girl asked her mother, Herodias, to help her decide what to ask for. Afraid that Herod would soon set John the Baptist free, she instructed the girl to ask for the head of John the Baptist on a platter. Herod was terribly disappointed to hear her make that request; nevertheless because of the oath he made before his guests, he had to grant Herodias daughter's request.

After that happened, John's disciples came and took John's body to bury it, and then they went and told Jesus.

Jesus was very sad to hear about the death of John the Baptist. Therefore, He wanted to go to a quiet place to rest a while, but a multitude of people tried to follow Him, and He had compassion on them. After He fed the multitude, He made His disciples take a boat to the other side of the sea, while He stayed behind to send the people away.

After the people left, Jesus went to a mountain to pray, being left alone on land.

Later that night Jesus walked on water, going to His disciples who were in the boat in the middle of the sea. When the disciples saw Him walking on water, they were afraid, thinking it was a ghost. Jesus said, "Be of good cheer, it is I; do not be afraid." Simon Peter answered, "Lord, if it is you, command me to come to you walking on water." Jesus answered and said, "Come." At first Peter walked on the water, but when he looked around and saw the terrible waves of the sea, he became afraid and started sinking. Immediately, Peter cried out and said the words that every sinner should say in their life time, "Lord save me!" And immediately Jesus stretched forth His hand and saved Peter, saying, "O thou of little faith, wherefore did you doubt?"

Jesus continued to heal many people. Among them was the woman who touched the hem of his garment, Jairus' daughter, the ten lepers, the man at the pool of Bethesda, and the man who had a legion of unclean spirits. The unclean spirits were subject unto Jesus, calling Him the Son of the most high God.

When the fame of Jesus' miracles spread throughout Israel, many thought that He was John the Baptist risen again from the dead. Others even thought that He was Elijah, Jeremiah, or one of the prophets in the Old Testament.

Jesus asked His disciples, "But who do you say that I am?" Simon Peter answered and said, "Thou art the Christ, the Son of the Living God." Jesus answered and said, "Blessed art thou, Simon Bar-jona: for flesh and blood hath not revealed it unto thee, but my Father which is in heaven. And I also say to you that you are Peter, and on this rock I will build my church, and the gates of hell shall not prevail against it. And I will give unto you the keys of the kingdom of heaven: and whatsoever you shall bind on earth shall be bound in heaven: and whatsoever you shall loose on earth shall be loosed in heaven."

Simon Peter felt good knowing that God had revealed Jesus' identity to him. But when Jesus began to speak about how He must die for our sins, Peter listened to the wrong voice and tried to stop Jesus from fulfilling His main purpose in coming to the earth. Therefore, Jesus rebuked Peter and said, "Get thee behind me, Satan! You are an offense unto me, for you are not mindful of things of God, but the things of men."

Knowing that Simon Peter was hurt from that rebuke, six days later Jesus took him, James and John with him unto a high mountain. On the mountain Jesus was transfigured before them. His face became as bright as the Sun, and his clothes were white as light.

And behold, Moses and Elijah appeared before them, talking with Jesus. Peter spoke and said, "Lord it is good for us to be here; if you wish, let us make here three tabernacles; one for you, one for Moses and one for Elijah," Suddenly, while Peter was still speaking, a bright cloud overshadowed them: and behold a voice came out of the cloud saying, "This is my beloved Son, in whom I am well pleased; hear ye Him."

The disciples became afraid, but after Jesus told them not to be afraid, He told them not to tell that vision to anyone until after His resurrection. His disciples asked Him about Elijah. Jesus answered and said. "Indeed Elijah is coming first and will restore all things. But I say unto you that Elijah had already come, and they did not know him, but did to him whatever they wished. Likewise shall also the Son of man suffer of them." Then at that time, they fully understood that he spoke to them about John the Baptist.

When Jesus healed on the Sabbath day, the Scribes and Pharisees became upset; when He said God was His father, they became furiously wroth and wanted to kill him because to them He not only had broken the Sabbath, but said also that God was his Father, making himself equal with God.

Jesus answered them and said, "I can of mine own self do nothing: as I hear, I judge; and my judgement is just; because I seek not mine own will, but the will of the Father which hath sent me. If I bear witness of myself, my witness is not true. There is another that beareth witness of me; and I know that the witness which he witnesseth of me is true. "You have sent unto John, and he bore witness unto the truth. But I receive not testimony from man; but these things I say, that you might be saved. He was a burning and a shining light: and you were willing for a season to rejoice in his light. But I have a greater witness than that of John: for the works which the Father hath given me to finish, the same works that I do, bear witness of me, that the Father hath sent me. And the Father Himself, which hath sent me, hath borne witness of me.

"You have neither heard his voice at any time, nor seen His shape. And you have not his word abiding in you; for whom He hath sent, Him you believe not. Search the scriptures; for in them ye think you have eternal life: and they are they which testify of me. And you will not come to me, that you might have life. I receive not honor from men. But I know you, that you have not the love of God in you. I am come in my Father's name, and you receive me not: if another shall come in his own name, him you will receive. How can you believe, which you receive honor one of another, and seek not the honor that comes from God only? "Do not think that I will accuse you to the Father: there is one that accuses you, even Moses in whom you trust. For had you believed Moses, you would have believed me; for he wrote of me; but if you believe not his writings, how shall you believe my words?"

Nevertheless, Jesus asked the Pharisees several questions that they couldn't answer. When they said that Christ was David's Son, He asked, "How then doth David in the spirit call him Lord, saying, The Lord said to my Lord, sit thou on my right hand, until I make thine enemies thy footstool? If David called him Lord, how is He his son?" They couldn't answer.

To the Sadducees, He said, "God is not the God of the dead, but the living." To the Herodians, He said, "Render therefore unto Caesar the things which are Caesar's; and unto God render therefore the things that are Gods." To the scribes He said, "Not that which goeth into the mouth defileth a man, but that which cometh out of the mouth, this defileth a man."

As for their question about the Sabbath day, He said, "What man shall there be among you that shall have one sheep, and if it fall into a pit on the Sabbath day, will he not lay hold on it, and lift out? How much then is a man better than a sheep? Wherefore it is lawful to do well on the Sabbath days. For the Son of man is Lord even of the Sabbath day."

Seeing that they had no answers to Jesus' questions, the Scribes and Pharisees tried to scare him away with fear by saying, "Get thee out, and depart hence; for Herod will kill thee." But Jesus calmly answered and said, "Go and tell that fox, behold, I cast out devils, and I did some healing today and tomorrow, and the third day I shall be complete before I leave. Nevertheless I must walk today, and tomorrow, and the day following; for it cannot be that a prophet perish out of Jerusalem."

Then after He gave the Scribes and Pharisees their many woes, He said, "You shall not see me again, until the time comes when you shall say, Blessed is He that comes in the name of the Lord."

To his disciples, Jesus said, "Not everyone that saith unto me, Lord, Lord, shall enter into the kingdom of heaven; but he that doeth the will of my Father which is in heaven. "Many will say in that day, Lord, Lord have we not prophesied in thy name? And in thy name have cast out devils? And in thy name done many wonderful works? And then will I profess unto them, I never knew you; depart from me, you that work iniquity."

Unto the good, he will say, "Well done thou good and faithful Servant. For I was hungry, and you gave me meat; I was thirsty, and you gave me drink; I was a stranger, and you took me in: I was in prison, and you came to see me. Then shall the righteous answer and say, Lord when did these things happen, and the King shall answer and say, inasmuch as you have done it unto one of the least of these my brethren, you have done it unto me."

The time came when Jesus had to break down the walls of prejudice between the Jews and Samaritans. He left Judaea, and departed again into Galilee. And he had to go through Samaria.

When He sat at Jacob's well because of His weary journey, a woman of Samaria came to draw water. "How is it that thou, being a Jew, ask me for a drink, which am a woman of Samaria? For the Jews have no dealing with the Samaritans," the woman grumbled when Jesus asked for a drink.

Jesus answered and said unto her, "If you knew the gift of God, and who it is that saith to thee, give me to drink; thou wouldest have asked of Him and He would have given thee living water." The woman was confused, therefore Jesus said, "Whosoever drinks of this well water shall thirst again; but whosoever drinks of the water that I shall give him shall never thirst; but the water that I shall give shall be in him a well of water springing up to everlasting life."

When the woman asked him about the appropriate place to worship God, Jesus answered and said, "Woman, believe me, the hour is coming, when ye shall neither in this mountain, nor yet at Jerusalem, worship the Father. You worship what you do not know; we know whom we worship for the salvation is of the Jews. But the hour is coming and now is, when the true worshipers will worship the Father in spirit and in truth; for the Father seeketh such to worship Him. God is a spirit; and they that worship Him must worship Him in spirit and in truth."

Just like the Jews, the woman and the rest of the Samaritans were still waiting for the coming of the messiah. Jesus revealed, "I who am speaking unto you, am He."

After Jesus fed thousands of his followers, he said, "Do not labor for the food which perishes, but for the food which endures unto everlasting life, which the Son of man shall give you; for him hath God the Father sealed."

"We will believe in you if you can make manna fall from heaven like Moses did," they replied.

Jesus answered and said, "Verily, verily I say unto you, Moses gave you not that bread from heaven; but my Father giveth you the true bread from heaven, for the bread of God is He which cometh down from heaven, and giveth life unto the world."

They said unto him, "Lord, evermore give us this bread." Jesus said unto them, "I am the bread of life: he that cometh to me shall never hunger; and he that believeth on me shall never thirst. But I said unto you, that ye also have seen me, and believe not.

"All that the Father giveth me shall come to me; and him that cometh to me I will in no wise cast out. For I came down from heaven, not to do mine own will, but the will of Him that sent me. And this is the Father's will which hath sent me, that of all which he hath given me I should lose nothing, but should raise it up again at the last day. And this is the will of Him that sent me that every one which seeth the Son, and believeth on Him, may have everlasting life; and I will raise Him up at the last day."

The Jews were confused, especially when Jesus said, "He that eateth my flesh, and drinketh my blood, dewelleth in me, and I in him."

Therefore many of His disciples when they heard this said, "This is a hard saying; who can understand it?" Jesus said, "No man can come to me, except the Father which hath sent me draw him; and I will raise him up at the last day. Therefore said I unto you; that no man come unto me, except it were given unto him of my Father."

From that time many of His disciples went back, and walked no more with Him. Then said Jesus unto the twelve, "Will you also go away?" Then Simon Peter answered Him, "Lord, to whom shall we go? Thou hast the words of eternal life, and we believe and are sure that thou art that Christ, the Son of the living God."

There was a question among the twelve about who should be the greatest in the kingdom of heaven? Jesus called a little child unto him, and sat him in the midst of them, and he said, "Verily I say unto you, except you be converted, and become as little children, ye shall not enter into the kingdom of heaven. Whosoever therefore shall humble himself as this little child, the same is the greatest in the kingdom of heaven and whoso shall receive one such little child in my name receiveth me. But whoso shall offend one of these little ones which believe in me, it were better for him that a millstone were hanged about his neck, and that he were drowned in the depth of the sea. Whosoever shall receive this child in my name receiveth me;

and whosoever shall receive me receiveth Him that sent me; for he that is least among you all, the same shall be great. But he that is greatest among you shall be your servant."

Jesus opened his mouth and taught his disciples lessons in parables. Among them were the parable of the forgiven servant who wouldn't forgive his fellow servant, the parable of the sower, the parable of the wheat and tares, the parable of the lost sheep, and the parable of a certain rich man who thought to himself saying, what shall I do, because I have no room where to bestow my fruit? And he said, this will I do; I will pull down my barns, and build greater; and there will I bestow all my fruits and my goods. And I will say to my soul, soul, thou hast much goods laid up for many years; take thine ease, eat, drink and be merry. But God said to him, thou fool, this night thy soul shall be required of thee; then whose shall those things be, which thou hast provided? So is he that layeth up treasure for himself, and is not rich toward God.

He also taught them how to pray saying, "Our Father which art in heaven, hallowed be thy name, Thy kingdom come, Thy will be done in earth, as it is in heaven; give us this day our daily bread. And forgive us our debts, as we forgive our debtors. And lead us not into temptation, but deliver us from evil: For thine is the kingdom, and the power, and the glory, forever. Amen."

Jesus told them, "All things, whatsoever ye shall ask in prayer, believing, ye shall receive.

"And I say unto you, ask, and it shall be given you: seek, and you shall find; knock, and it shall be opened. If a son shall ask bread of any of you that is a father, will he give him a stone? Or if he ask a fish, will he for fish give him a serpent? Or if he shall ask an egg, will he offer him a scorpion? If ye then, being evil, know how to give good gifts unto your children, how much more shall your heavenly Father give the Holy Spirit to them that ask Him?"

Many people said, "John did no miracle; but all things that John spoke about this man were true," and many believed on Him there.

When Jesus was told that Lazarus was sick, he said, "This sickness is not unto death, but for the glory of God, that the Son of God might be glorified thereby." Knowing that He was going to raise Lazarus from the grave, He said, "Our friend Lazarus sleepeth; but I go, that I may awake him out of sleep."

"Lord, if thou had been here, my brother had not died," Martha said to Jesus when He arrived in town. Jesus said to her, "Thy brother shall rise again." Martha said, "I know that he shall rise again in the resurrection at the last day." Jesus said unto her, "I am the resurrection, and the life; he that believeth in me, though he were dead, yet shall he live; and whosoever liveth and believeth in me shall never die. Believeth thou this?" She said, "Yes, Lord; I believe that thou art the Christ, the Son of God, which should come into the world." With Martha and Mary watching, Jesus ordered the people to take away the stone. When they did, Jesus lifted his eyes to heaven and said, "Father, I thank thee that thou hast heard me, and I know that thou hearest me always; but because of the people which stand by, I said it, that they may believe that thou hast sent me."

And when He thus had spoken, He cried with a loud voice, "Lazarus come forth!" and immediately Lazarus came forth alive again.

When Jesus went to eat at the house of a Pharisee name Simon, a certain sinful woman came and anointed Him with an alabaster box, kissing His feet and washing them with the tears of her eyes, and drying them with her hair. "This man, if He was a prophet, would have known who and what manner of woman this is that touched Him; for she is a sinner," Simon thought to himself.

After reproaching Simon for not showing compassion and genuine hospitality, Jesus said to the woman, "Your sins, which are many, are forgiven."

Judas got angry because she used the expensive ointment on Jesus. "Leave her alone; against the day of my burying hath she kept this. For the poor always you have with you, but me you have not always," Jesus said.

When the time came for Jesus to make his triumphal entry into Jerusalem, He said to two of His disciples, "Go ye into the village over against you; in the which at your entering ye shall find a colt tied whereon yet never man sat; loose him, and bring him hither. And if any man ask you, why do you loose him? Thus shall ye say unto him, because the Lord hath need of him." They went their way and did as Jesus had told them.

When Jesus entered Jerusalem, riding on a colt, the mass of people spread their clothes and palm branches, shouting, Hosanna: Blessed is He that cometh in the name of the Lord: Blessed be the kingdom of our Father David, that cometh in the name of the Lord: Hosanna in the highest.

When the Pharisees heard this, they responded and said to Jesus, "Master rebuke thy disciples." And Jesus answered and said, "I tell you that, if these should hold their peace, the stones would immediately cry out."

When the chief priests and scribes heard the little children saying, "Hosanna to the Son of David," they were so displeased. Jesus answered and said, "Yea: have you never read, out of the mouth of babes and suckling thou hast perfected praise?"

When Jesus went into the temple of God, He saw them selling and buying merchandise. Jesus overturned the tables of the money changers and cried, "It is written, my house shall be called the house of prayer, but ye have made it a den of thieves."

"With what authority doest thou these things, and who gave thee this authority?" they asked Jesus.

He answered and said, "I also will ask you one thing, which if you tell me, I in like wise will tell you by what authority I do these things. The baptism of John, whence was it, from heaven or of man?" They reasoned and said to themselves, "If we shall say from heaven; he will say, why did you not then believe him? But if we shall say, of men; we fear the people; for all hold John the Baptist as a prophet." Therefore they answered and said, "We cannot tell." Jesus said, "Neither I tell you by what authority I do these things. But what think ye? A certain man had two sons; and he came to the first, and said, Son, go work today in my vineyard. He answered and said, I will not: but afterward he repented, and went. And he came to the second, and said likewise, and he answered and said, I go sir: and went not. Which of the two did the will of his father?" They answered and said, "The first."

Jesus said unto them, "Verily I say unto you, that the publicans and the harlots go into the kingdom of God before you. For John came unto you as the way of righteousness, and ye believed him not: but the publicans and harlots believed him: and ye, when you had seen it, repented not afterwards, that you might believe in him."

The Pharisees sought to lay hands on Jesus, but they feared the people who considered Jesus a prophet, nevertheless they asked again, "What sign showest thou us, that thou do these things?" Jesus answered and said, "Destroy this temple, and in three days I will raise it up." They answered, "Forty—six years it took to build this temple, and you would raise it up in three days?" But Jesus was speaking about the temple of his body. Yet he asked them who were trusting in their gold and gifts in the temple, which was greater, the gold, or the temple that sanctifith the gold? Or, what was greater, the gift or the altar that sanctifith the gift?

"What shall I do to inherit eternal life?" A lawyer asked, tempting Jesus. Jesus said, "Thou shalt love the Lord thy God with all thy heart, and with all thy soul, and with all thy mind. And Thou shalt love thy neighbor as thyself. On these two commandments hang all the law and the prophets."

"Who is my neighbor?" the lawyer asked. Jesus told him the parable of the good samaritan who had more mercy and compassion for the wounded man than the priest and Levite. "Go, and do likewise," Jesus said.

A rich young ruler who said he had kept all of God's commandments from his youth wanted to know how he could have eternal life. "One thing you lack: go and sell all you have to the poor, and you shall have treasures in heaven: and come, take up your cross and follow me," Jesus answered.

The man walked away sorrowful for he was very rich. When Jesus saw that the man was sorrowful, He said, "It is easier for a camel to go through the eye of a needle, than for a rich man to enter into the kingdom of God." "Who then can be saved?" they asked Jesus. "With men it is impossible, but with God all things are possible," He answered. Then He said to the disciples, "If any man will come after me, let him deny himself; and take up his cross, and follow me. For whosoever will save his life shall lose it: and whosoever will lose his life for my sake shall find it. For what is a man profited, if he shall gain the whole world, and lose his own soul? Or what shall a man give in exchange for his soul?"

"How often should I forgive one who did me wrong?" His disciples asked. "Not just seven times, but seventy times seven," Jesus answered. He told them the parable of the prodigal son to whom mercy and forgiveness was shown, then he told them the story of the rich man and Lazarus, to let them know what will happen when you don't show mercy and forgiveness toward someone.

He also told his disciples that He was the true vine, and the Good Shepherd. He told them, "I am the way, the truth, and the life! No man cometh unto the Father, but by me."

Jesus looked and saw rich men giving their gifts into the treasury, and He also saw a certain poor widow giving her two mites. Then He said, "Of a truth, I say unto you, that this poor widow has gave more than they all; for all these have of their abundance given, but she of want did cast in all that she had, even all her living."

"Behold your mother and brothers are here wishing to speak with you," they told Jesus.

"Who is my mother? And who are my brothers?" he asked them. He stretched forth his hand toward his disciples and said, "Behold my mother and my brothers! For whosoever shall do the will of my Father which is in heaven, the same is my brother, and sister, and mother."

To tempt Him and to accuse Him, the Scribes and Pharisees brought unto Him a woman taken in adultery. "Now Moses in the law commanded us to stone her, but what do you say?" they asked. After Jesus stooped down and wrote on the ground He lifted Himself back up and said, "He that is without sin among you, let him first cast a stone at her." Being convicted in their hearts, they all left, until it was only Jesus and the woman remaining. "Woman, where are your accusers? Hath no man condemned thee?" He asked. She said, "No man Lord." Jesus said, "Neither do I condemn you, go and sin no more."

There was a man who was blind from his birth. Jesus' disciples asked him, "Master, who did sin, this man or his parents, that he was born blind?" Jesus answered, "Neither hath this man sinned, nor his parents; but that the work of God should be made manifest in him. I must work the works of Him that sent me, while it is day: the night cometh, when no man can work. As long as I'm in the world, I am the light of the world." After Jesus made clay from His spittle, He put it on the blind man's eyes, and He told him to go wash in the pool of Siloam. The blind man obeyed Him and he came back seeing. The Pharisees didn't want to believe Jesus gave sight to the blind man, nor did some of them believe the man's parents who testified that the man was indeed born blind. "Give God the praise: we know that this man is a sinner," the Pharisees said to the blind man. "Whether he be a sinner or not, I know not; one thing I know, that I was born blind, but now I see," the man answered.

"You can be His disciple, but we are Moses' disciples," they said to him. The man answered and said, "We know that God does not listen to sinners, but if any man be a worshipper of God, and doeth His will, him will God hear. Since the world began nobody opened the eyes of one that was born blind; if this man was not of God, he could do nothing." "You were altogether born in sin, yet you are trying to teach us?" they said before they threw him out of the temple.

When Jesus heard that they threw him out, He found him and asked, "Do you believe on the Son of God?" "Who is he Lord that I might believe on him?" the man replied. "Not only have you seen Him, but He is talking with you right now," Jesus answered. "Lord, I believe." The man replied. And he immediately worshipped Jesus. Jesus said, "For Judgment I come into this world to give sight to those who cannot see; and to take away sight from those who can."

Some of the Pharisees, which were there, heard him and replied, "Are we blind also?" Jesus answered and said unto them, "If you were blind you would be without sin, but since you say you see, therefore your sin remaineth." The Pharisees were in full rage. Jesus said, "There will not be left one stone upon another, because you knew not the time of your visitation. The stone which the builders rejected, the same is become the head corner. Whosoever shall fall upon that stone shall be broken, but on whomsoever it shall fall, it will grind him to powder."

They had had enough; they thought that Jesus was a blasphemer. First they heard Him say, "Before Abraham was I am," then they heard Him say, "I and my Father are one," and now this! They immediately thought of ways to have Him killed. Yet Jesus, knowing all things, knew that His time was at hand. Therefore He said, "The hour is come, that the Son of man should be glorified."

Again, He said, "Father, glorify your name." Then came a voice from heaven saying, "I have both glorified it, and will glorify it again."

The people who heard the voice thought it either thundered or an angel spoke to Him. Jesus answered and said, "This voice came not because of me, but for your sakes. Now is the judgment of this world; now shall the prince of this world be cast out. And I, if I be lifted up from the earth, will draw all men unto me."

Knowing that it was the night that He would be betrayed, Jesus ate the Passover with his twelve Apostles. "Verily I say unto you that one of you shall betray me," Jesus said to the twelve. They were sorrowful and they all asked Him, "Lord is it I?" Jesus said, "He that dippeth his hand with me in the dish, the same shall betray me. The Son of man goeth as it is written of Him: but woe unto that man by whom the Son of man is betrayed! It had been good for that man if he had not been born."

"Master, is it I?" Judas asked. "You said it," Jesus answered. Then entered Satan into Judas. Jesus said unto him, "That thou doest; do quickly." And immediately Judas left.

As they were eating, Jesus took bread, and blessed it, and broke it, and gave it to the disciples, saying, "Take eat, this is my body." And He took the cup, and gave thanks, and gave it to them, saying, "Drink ye all of it, for this is my blood of the new testament, which is shed for many for the remission of sins. But I say unto you, I will not drink henceforth of this fruit of the vine, until that day when I drink it new with you in my Father's kingdom."

When Jesus started washing His disciples feet, Simon Peter tried to forbid Him, but Jesus answered and said, "If I wash thee not, thou hast no part with me." Peter immediately allowed Him to wash his feet. "If I then, your Lord and Master, have washed your feet, ye also ought to wash one another's feet. For I have given you an example, that you should do as I have done to you."

Then said Jesus, "Little children, yet a little while I am with you, you shall seek me, and as I said unto the Jews, where I go, you cannot come; so now I say to you, a new commandment I give to you, that you love one another; as I loved you, that you also love one another. By this shall all men know that you are my disciples, if you have love one to another."

Simon Peter said to Jesus, "Lord, why cannot I follow you now? I will lay down my life for your sake." Jesus answered him, "Will you lay down your life for my sake? Verily, verily I say unto you, the cock shall not crow, till thou hast denied me three times."

Seeing that His disciples were sad, Jesus continued and said, "Let not your heart be troubled; ye believe in God, believe also in me. In my Father's house are many mansions, if it were not so, I would have told you. I go to prepare a place for you, And if I go and prepare a place for you, I will come again, and receive you unto myself, that where I am, there you may be also."

Seeing that His apostles were still a little sad, Jesus said, "If you love me, keep my commandments. And I will pray to the Father, and He shall give you another Comforter, that He may abide with you forever; even the Spirit of truth, whom the world cannot receive, because it sees Him not, neither knoweth Him. But you know Him; for he dwells with you, and shall be in you. I will not leave you comfortless: I will come to you. But the Comforter, which is the Holy Ghost, whom the Father will send in my name, He shall teach you all things, and bring all things to your remembrance, whatsoever I have said unto you."

Then Jesus lifted up His eyes to heaven and said, "Father the hour is come; glorify thy Son, that thy Son also may glorify you."

Again He said, "And now, O Father, glorify me together with yourself, with the glory which I had with you before the world was," and again He said, "And the glory which you gave me I have given them, that they may be one just as we are one; I in them, and you in me that they may be made perfect in one, and that the world may know that you have sent me, and have loved them as you have loved me. Father I will that they also whom you gave me may be with me where I am, that they may behold my glory which you have given me; for you loved me before the foundation of the world.

"O righteous Father! The world has not known you, but I have known you; and these have known that you sent me."

And after they all sang a hymn, they went out into the Mount of Olives.

Jesus said to His disciples, "Sit here, while I go and pray yonder." He took Peter, James and John with Him a little further, and then he said to them, "My soul is exceeding sorrowful, even unto death: wait here, and watch with me." And He went a little further, and fell on His face, and prayed, saying, "O my Father, if it be possible, let this cup pass from me, nevertheless not as I will, but as thou wilt." When He came to the disciples, He found them asleep, and He said to Peter, "What, could you not watch with me one hour? Watch and pray that you enter not into temptation, The Spirit indeed is willing, but the flesh is weak."

Then Jesus went again the second time, and prayed saying, "O my Father, if this cup may not pass away from me, except I drink it, your will be done." Once again He went and found his disciples sleep, therefore He went back and prayed the third time. When He came back to the disciples He said, "Sleep on now, and take your rest. Behold, the hour is at hand, and the Son of man is being betrayed into the hands of sinners." Judas led a multitude of soldiers to Jesus. Giving them the sign, Judas draw near Jesus to kiss Him. Jesus said unto Judas, "Judas, betrayest thou the Son of man with a kiss?"

In the midst of the commotion, Peter drew a sword and cut off the right ear of the high priest's servant. After Jesus ordered Peter to put up the sword, he healed the man's ear.

Just as Jesus had foretold, all his disciples forsook Him and fled. Yet Peter followed at a distance, and so did John the son of Zebedee. While Peter warmed himself by the fire, he was recognized three times, and each time he denied that he even knew Jesus. Immediately, like Jesus foretold, the cock crowed; at that moment, Peter remembered Jesus' words, and he went out and cried bitterly.

Jesus stood before the chief priests while several of the Pharisees struggled to find a reason to agree to put Jesus to death. Finally there arose certain false witnesses saying, "We heard Him say He will destroy this temple made with hands and within three days build another one without hands."

Finally the high priest asked Jesus, "Are you the Christ, the Son of the living God?" Jesus answered and said, "I am. And you shall see the Son of man sitting on the right hand of power and coming in the clouds of heaven." The high priest tore his clothes, and said, "We don't need any further witness. We just heard his blasphemy."

When Judas realized that they had condemned Jesus to death, he returned the thirty pieces of silver to the chief priest and elders, saying, "I have sinned and betrayed innocent blood." He threw the pieces of silver in the temple and ran off and hanged himself.

The chief priest took Jesus to Pontius Pilate, who was the governor of Judea.

Before him the Jews accused Jesus of claiming to be the king of the Jews, hoping that Pilate would think Jesus was guilty of treason against Caesar. Pilate asked Jesus, "Are you the king of the Jews?" Jesus answered and said, "You said it." Again He said, "My kingdom is not of this world. If my kingdom was of this world, then would my servants fight that I should not be delivered to the Jews. But now my kingdom is not from here." Pilate answered and asked, "Are you a king then?" Jesus answered, "You can say I am a king. For this cause I was born, and for this cause I am come into the world, that I should bear witness unto the truth. Every one that is of the truth hears my voice."

When Pilate heard that Jesus was from Galilee, he sent Him to Herod who was in Jerusalem. Herod wanted to see Jesus perform miracles, but Jesus did not respond to Herod. Therefore Herod sent Him back to Pilate.

Pilate told the chief priest that after examining Jesus, he couldn't find fault in Him, so he decided to whip Jesus, then let Him go.

Jesus was severely whipped, but the chief priest wouldn't let Pilate release him, saying, "Away with this man. Crucify Him, crucify Him, He claims to be the Son of God."

When Pilate heard that he became afraid, and asked Jesus, "Who are you?" But Jesus didn't answer. Then Pilate said, "What, you are not speaking to me? Don't you know that I have the power to crucify you, and the power to release you?" Jesus answered and said, "You could have no power at all against me, except it was given to you from above; therefore the ones who delivered me to you have the greater sin."

Some of the same people who had hailed Jesus when He rode into Jerusalem a few days earlier, now turned on Him. When Pilate gave the people the choice between Jesus and Barabbas, they shouted, "Away with this man and release unto us Barabbas!" Therefore Pilate gave into their request and ordered Jesus to be crucified. They stripped Jesus and put on Him a scarlet robe, and they put on his head a crown of thorns. And bearing His cross, Jesus was led to Golgotha Hill. Being too weary to continue on the journey, Jesus' cross was carried by Simon of Cyrene. Jesus was crucified between two thieves.

Nailed to the cross, Jesus said, "Father, forgive them for they know not what they do."

To Mary he said, "Woman, behold your Son."

To John he said, "Behold your mother." At that moment, John knew that Jesus wanted him to take care of Mary like a mother.

Because Jesus took upon Himself all the sins of the world, the sky turned dark. Jesus cried out to God, "Eli, Eli lama sabachthami?" which is to say "My God, My God why has thou forsaken me?"

One of the thieves repented and asked Jesus to remember him when He come into His kingdom. Being a savior, even when He was dying, Jesus said to the thief, "Today you shall be with me in paradise."

Becoming thirsty, Jesus said, "I thirst." They filled a sponge with vinegar and gave it to Jesus.

Jesus cried with a loud voice, "Father, into thy hands I commend my spirit. It is finished." He immediately hung His head and died.

And behold, the veil of the temple was torn in two pieces, from top to bottom. And there was an earthquake. And the graves opened, and many bodies of saints arose from the dead, as Jesus spiritually went to get them, saying, "Lift up your heads, o ye gates; and be ye lift up ye everlasting doors; and the king of glory shall come in."

But that's not how the story ends; after three days Jesus rose again.

Very early on the first day of the week, the Marys went to Jesus tomb to anoint His body, but they found that He was already risen.

"Touch me not; for I am not yet ascended to my Father, but go to my brethren, and say unto them, I ascend unto my Father, and your Father; and to my God, and your God," Jesus said to the women after they recognized Him. Full of joy the women ran and told the Apostles.

And behold, two men walked on the road to Emmaus that same day. While they talked, Jesus Himself drew near them and asked, "What manner of communications are these that you have one to another, as you walk, and are sad?" One of them, named Cleopas, answered and said, "Are you only a stranger in Jerusalem and hast not known the things which are come to pass there in these days?" "What things?" Jesus asked. After the man went into details, confirming that the first day of the week was indeed the third day since those things was done, Jesus said, "O fools, and slow of heart to believe all that the prophets have spoken.

"Ought not Christ to have suffered these things and to enter into His glory?" And beginning with Moses and all the prophets, Jesus expounded to them the scriptures concerning Himself.

"Abide with us, for it is toward evening, and the day is far spent," they said, asking Jesus to spend time with them, although they still didn't know Him. When they finally did, He vanished out of their sight. And they said, "Did not our heart burn within us, while He talked with us by the way, and while He opened to us the scriptures?"

When Jesus appeared to the apostles, they were afraid; He said unto them, "Why are you troubled? And why do thoughts arise in your hearts? Behold my hands and my feet, that it is I myself; handle me and see, for a spirit have not flesh and bones, as you see me have." To Thomas he said, "Be not faithless but believing." Thomas answered and said, "My Lord and my God." Jesus said, "Thomas, because you have seen me, you believed: blessed are they that have not seen, yet believed."

Finally He told them all, "These are the words which I spoke unto you, while I was yet with you, that all things must be fulfilled, which were written in the law of Moses, and in the prophets, and in the psalms, concerning me." Then He opened their understanding that they might understand the scripture and He said unto them. "Thus it is written, and thus it behooved Christ to suffer, and to rise from the dead the third day; and that repentance and remission of sins should be preached in His name among all nations, beginning in Jerusalem. And you are witness of these things. And behold, I send the promise of my Father upon you: but wait in the city of Jerusalem, until you be endued with power from on high."

Again Jesus said, "All power is given unto me in heaven and in earth. Go ye therefore, and teach all nations, baptizing them in the name of the Father, and of the Son, and of the Holy Ghost." Again He said, "He that believeth and is baptized shall be saved; but he that believeth not shall be condemned. And these signs shall follow them that believe; in my name shall they cast out devils: they shall speak with new tongues; they shall take up serpents; and if they drink any deadly thing, it shall not hurt them. They shall lay hands on the sick, and they shall recover."

Again He told them, "For John truly baptized with water, but you shall be baptized with the Holy Ghost not many days from now."

Then He blessed them, and while He blessed them, He was carried up into heaven. And the disciples saw Him go up to heaven. And two angels said to them, "Why are you looking up at heaven? This same Jesus will come back the same way He left you." And the disciples returned to Jerusalem, and were continually in the temple praising and blessing God. As for Jesus, He is now alive forevermore, and is sitting at the right hand of the Father. If we be good people, soon and very soon, He will come back for us so we can spend eternity with Him in heaven.

In conclusion, you may find many great prophets and Biblical characters who can say they did God's will, but none of them would dare say that they are greater than the Lord Jesus, and only one had the privilege of being born the same year as Jesus. No one can be compared to them. John is the greatest born of woman, but even he is subject to Jesus, because in the beginning was the Word, who is Jesus, the Son of God.

Again, both were born on this earth the same year, and both was sent to reconcile man back to God at about the same time. John came to prepare our hearts, but Jesus came to save us and live in our hearts. For greater is He that is in you than He that is in the world.

The End

The very next morning, little Tommy got up bright and early with joy.

"Wow, that was a great story you told me last night, Grandma," he said.

"I know, I know," Grandma answered, "Now go wash, brush your teeth and freshen up for breakfast."

"No offense Grandma but I am not all that hungry this morning," Tommy answered. "I cannot live by food alone, but by every word that comes out of the mouth of God. I have been feeding my soul this morning, and my soul is already full."

"No problem at all," Rose answered. "I am very happy to see that the Lord Jesus touched your heart last night; and that He put it on your heart to fast this morning."

"He sure did; in a very special way." Tommy answered.

After a brief moment of silence, he exhaled and said, "I think I know what I want to be when I grow up."

"What is that?" Both Rose and Midas asked.

"I want to be like John the Baptist," Tommy answered. "I want to help prepare the way for Jesus' second coming. I want to be a servant of God and mankind. "Yes, it would be nice to be a rapper, a singer, a tennis player, a basketball player, a fighter, a preacher, a doctor, lawyer, teacher or even President of the United States; all those careers are great, but no matter what I may become, as long as the Lord allows me to be a humbled servant, I will be happy, because He that is greatest among you shall be your servant."

Overwhelmed with joy, Midas and Rose answered and said together, "Amen."

The End